FINANCIALLY FIT
for life

To our families and everyone who has supported us
through the writing of this book

FINANCIALLY FIT
for life

Frances Beck, Emily Chantiri,
Dianne Hill, Di Robinson

RANDOM HOUSE AUSTRALIA

The information set out in this book is not intended to be taken or relied upon as specific investment or financial advice. The authors and the publisher shall not be liable in respect of any claim arising out of reliance on the information in this book. All information, including prices, interest rates and laws, is, as far as the authors can ascertain, correct at the time of writing. Readers should always obtain independent or other professional advice before acting, as everyone's circumstances are different and the law does change.

The names of some interviewees have been changed to protect their privacy.

Random House Australia Pty Ltd
20 Alfred Street, Milsons Point, NSW 2061
http://www.randomhouse.com.au

Sydney New York Toronto
London Auckland Johannesburg

First published by Random House Australia 2003
Copyright © Emily Chantiri, Frances Beck, Dianne Hill, Di Robinson 2003

National Library of Australia
Cataloguing-in-Publication Entry

Financially fit for life.

ISBN 1 74051 184 0.

1. Finance, Personal. I. Beck, Frances.

640.42

Cover photograph: Stock Photos
Cover design by Darian Causby/Highway 51
Typeset in 11.5/13.5 Adobe Garamond by Midland Typesetters, Maryborough, Victoria
Printed and bound by Griffin Press, Netley, South Australia

10 9 8 7 6 5 4 3 2 1

Contents

Introduction

Five years ago when we started an investment club, little did we know that this small venture was about to change our lives. Back then, our idea was to get together with like-minded friends and learn about investing and the stock market. Our group consisted of well-educated women, but surprisingly, when it came to investing or talking about money, we were at a loss.

Even our resident accountant, Dianne Hill, had reservations about investing because of a previous bad experience. So we set about changing our attitudes and learning about the world of finance. At that time, Emily Chantiri was the only one of us who had started investing in the share market, using the internet to buy and sell shares. The rest of us did not know where to start learning about the stock market, and did not have enough time to work it out.

In our club, it took some time to do just that, compounded by the lack of information available about setting up a club, but after six months we finally bought our first share. By pooling our resources, we learned a lot about investing in shares and we had a lot of fun in the process. Friends and colleagues who knew about our club were keen to join or even start a club of their own. There was a lot of interest, but little information. There were plenty of financial books, but none seemed to really deal with investment clubs. This is where the idea came from to write our first book, *The Money Club*, an easy and simple guide to starting an investment club.

If starting an investment club was an eye-opener, then the feedback we received after launching *The Money Club* was even more enlightening. Why? Like us, many of our readers wanted to take control of their finances, but didn't know where to start or why they hadn't done so. What became apparent to us was that a person cannot expect to start investing if they do not understand the reasons holding them back in the first place. The underlying reasons or excuses we heard from readers were not dissimilar to our own. In *Financially Fit for Life* we tackle these issues, from our inherited attitudes and fears through to excuses such as not having enough time.

When we spoke at various events, people could relate to our stories. We are normal people, juggling careers and families, and we are not financial wizards. We mentioned earlier that Dianne Hill is a chartered accountant, but had not been an active investor. Frances Beck is a lawyer, Di Robinson works in the corporate world and Emily Chantiri is a writer in the advertising industry.

Certainly, having children was another good reason for us to secure our financial future. Today, five years after first deciding to take the plunge and start an investment club, we still openly discuss our own finances and ways we can save money, even if it's just using each other as a sounding board for advice.

In *Financially Fit for Life*, you'll hear our stories about other investments we have made over the past few years. Dianne started her own superannuation fund, and Di, Frances and Emily have bought investment properties. In simple terms, we'll explain the processes involved in each of these ventures, and we'll help you understand the benefits of setting goals, building wealth, general investing, superannuation, being aware of legal issues, and protecting yourself.

You don't have to be a financial expert to take control of your money. The case studies in this book are our stories and stories from colleagues and friends; ordinary people who have successfully learned what they needed to do to become financially fit. You'll hear about their decisions, and the steps they followed when taking control of their finances. Their actions may help you in your own life. You'll discover that you are not alone. We thank them for their generosity in sharing their stories and for being a source of inspiration.

The path to financial fitness is in many ways similar to physical fitness. Just as anyone can improve their physical fitness, with a little work anyone can improve his or her financial fitness. It's a question of setting goals and working out what you have to do to achieve them. The best way to do this is in small chunks, working towards a target. We know it's easy to get sidetracked, as we have all been there. Just remember, one step at a time.

Becoming financially fit gives you more choices and options without feeling guilty or carrying the heavy burden of being in debt for the rest of your life. It's not just about having more money as an end in itself, it's about being able to live the life you really want. Imagine taking the trip of a lifetime or having time off to study something you've always longed to do. If you're financially fit, these will be your goals, not your dreams.

For us, there has been no greater reward than inspiring others to start their own investment club or take action to build and secure their own financial position. If we can do it, along with many others who have moved from being financially challenged to financially fit, then so can you.

Emily, Frances, Dianne and Di

CHAPTER 1

What's holding you back?

We all have issues to deal with that act as barriers to becoming financially fit. These barriers could come from the attitudes we inherit from our families, our deep-seated fears and anxieties, or maybe from the main curse of modern life: not having enough time to fit everything in! Don't despair, there are plenty of ways over these barriers, as you'll find out in this chapter.

Our inherited attitudes

What better place to start than right at the very beginning. We all know there are lots of things we've inherited from our parents that we can't change – being too short or tall, having curly or straight hair, freckles, etc. But there are other things we inherit that aren't in our genes: our attitudes. When we were young our parents were our role models. They provided an environment for our growth; they clothed, fed and educated us. We relied on their judgement to help us through our growing years.

So it goes without question that when it comes to financial matters, our attitudes towards money have also been strongly influenced by our parents. If you grew up in a household where your parents struggled and had to watch every penny, then it is understandable that you will probably have picked up some of their traits, in contrast to someone who grew up with an abundance of money. But unlike the physical attributes given to us by our parents, we can change our attitudes and values towards our finances.

We know change is possible because we have all heard the 'rags to riches' stories. But before we can help you move on to taking control of your finances, it is important to understand the reasons why you haven't done so in the past or why you haven't been able to change.

When we launched our first book, *The Money Club*, we spoke to many people who were like us. They wanted to learn about investing, but found they could not move ahead or take the first leap forward. The common underlying thread was the 'excuses'; the very same lines we were using before we set out on our journey to become financially fit.

Take a look at the statements below – do you identify with any of them? We certainly did.

- I worry that I'm not saving any money.
- I don't know where my money goes every month.
- I can't pay the full balance on my credit card(s).
- I seem to be getting into more and more debt.
- I don't have time to organise my finances.
- Books and articles on financial topics have too much jargon and are hard to understand.
- I'm worried that I'll be ripped off.
- I don't know where to start.

The list goes on, but you can see that there are many perceived barriers holding us back. In writing this book, we authors spent many hours discussing our own finances. These discussions helped us enormously because we realised we were not alone.

It's definitely worth looking at some of the issues that have shaped your own attitudes to money. Money attitudes stem from our earliest memories in childhood. Perhaps you grew up in a household where money was never talked about, or even considered a socially unacceptable topic. These attitudes influence your career choices, how you save and invest, and what sorts of risks you are prepared to take.

Think back to when you were growing up as you read the following questions. Which questions might reflect why you haven't been able to move on or change your beliefs?

- Did your parents save money?
- What are the conversations you can remember around money? For example: 'Money doesn't grow on trees.' 'You don't need new shoes; you already have a pair.' 'We don't have enough money to feed the family and you want something for yourself?'
- Were you involved in financial discussions?
- Were you encouraged to be financially self-reliant, or did you rely on others to bail you out?
- Did your family give you pocket money and encourage you to learn to manage money and save?
- Were your parents frightened of taking risks with money?
- Were your parents irresponsible with money?
- Did you see your parents making or losing a great deal of money? Did the change affect your family's lifestyle?

Almost no one is neutral about money. We generally have various belief systems or values attached to money. For example, do you agree that banks are safe places to invest money? Or that investing in shares is a good way to build wealth? Or do you think investing in shares is like gambling? Where do these beliefs come from? Are they from your experiences as an adult, or are they the opinions of your family, remembered and absorbed from childhood? Are your beliefs the opposite of your parents' as a reaction against the ideas you grew up with?

If you came from a family where nothing was ever saved and money was always spent without thought, you may find it difficult to plan for what you want to buy and set up a saving system of some kind. You may not even associate the fact that you are not where you want to be with your lack of a savings plan – you might think that you *have* to spend every pay just to meet your everday needs, when in fact it is your attitude keeping you from saving, and not a lack of money.

If you were never involved in any financial discussions when you were growing up you may not have a sense of how to talk about money planning. You may need to start with learning the 'finance' vocabulary before starting to plan anything.

Michael was brought up in a household where money was freely talked about. He has seen the effect of financial successes and failures in his own family.

Until I was 17 I had a fairly privileged upbringing. My siblings and I went to private schools and we were lucky to live in one of Sydney's exclusive waterside suburbs.

My father and his brothers were all well educated, winning scholarships to major universities. Education and success were extremely important on my father's side of the family. Whenever we got together with my father's family they openly talked about money and what ventures they were into. My mother's side was quite different; they were middle class and money wasn't such a 'force' as it was with my dad's family. I can recall that at family gatherings the members of my mother's family would steer clear of my dad's; they clearly thought money should not be discussed.

My father's business had been going really well, until he got caught up in a bank that lost its money due to an affiliation with the collapsed Pyramid group. My father had obtained a loan from this bank to build a substantial block of apartments. Halfway through, the bank collapsed, leaving my father with massive debts. Now he had to repay his debts, and the bank had no money to give him.

This meant he had to sell all our assets and he was declared bankrupt. We were saved from losing everything because the family home was in my parents' joint names. My mother fought the banks to keep her half. After a lengthy court case she won the right to keep her home.

This went on for several years, and really took its toll on my father. My dad was in financial trouble and could not chase his debtors. He didn't have money to take them to court; they knew he could not chase them, so they never paid him back. Not long before this collapse, my parents had talked about trust funds, but unfortunately they never did anything about it.

I'm now in my late twenties and the lesson for me is that when you have money you have to find some way to secure it. You need a fallback position. Because of what happened to my father, I worry more. I'm also more aggressive because I know what I missed when my father lost all his money. I'm aiming and working to get back what I missed when everything collapsed from under us.

Michael learnt a valuable lesson when he saw his father's business collapse. This came not only from the financial loss, but also from the effect on his family when they almost lost their family home. He is adamant that the mistakes his father made will not happen to him.

Safety and security

We all have our own childhood memories; Dianne Hill shares her story with us.

Dianne's parents were like many who had gone through the Depression. The strong values they tried to instil in her were hard work, safety and security. Dianne worked hard from a young age, but initially reacted against her parents' insistence on safety and security.

I started full-time work when I was 15, in an office. When I was 17 I received a payout from a car accident. 'Buy a block of land,' said my dad. But I wanted to make my own decisions; I was at an age where I didn't want to do anything my parents said. Instead, I just frittered the money away, and in a few years the block of land I should have bought trebled in value. When I was 19, I married, and we built a house. When that marriage came to an end, my husband bought me out, but again I just spent the money instead of investing it.

Then came another accident payout and, after losing half of it to my then boyfriend (another nightmare story), I at least put what I had left into another house, which also trebled in value.

When I met my next partner he encouraged me to buy a house near where he lived, then I sold that and we bought a house together as tenants in common. I was careful to protect my half share, which I owned outright, from my partner's half, which was mortgaged. When that relationship broke up my first thought was that we would have to sell the house and split the proceeds, but after looking around at what I could buy, I decided to take out a mortgage and buy my partner out. This was a big risk, as I didn't have a job at the time, but it was calculated, as I knew that if it all went wrong I had a substantial asset to sell. The risk was well taken as I got the job I wanted, I am now paying off my mortgage and my property's value has increased by one-third in two years.

I realise that I have now finally put into practice the values my parents were trying to instil in me when I was a teenager. My house is increasing in value all the time, and I feel financially secure.

It's hard to take advice from our parents, particularly as teenagers and young adults. Now, after some years, Dianne can see that her parents' advice was in her best interest.

Overcoming low expectations

To be financially successful requires a reasonably high level of self-esteem. You need to have confidence in yourself. This can be hard if you come from a family where there are no role models, and low expectations. On the other hand, as Brian's story shows, this kind of background can give you a real incentive to improve things, and a 'nothing to lose' attitude with regard to risk-taking.

Brian grew up in a very poor family. His family did not have any money to save and he didn't do well at school. He did not have any role models to follow. He was set to follow the experiences of his family and friends – to move onto the dole and get occasional low-skilled work. However, Brian found a job in a bank and this broke him away from his past. He flourished in the workplace and worked hard. He was recognised and encouraged by his managers and this changed things for him.

I grew up in a family of nine children. We lived in housing commission flats and my father died when I was seven. I lived with a number of relatives while I was growing up as my mother struggled to keep the children fed and clothed. My clothes came from the Smith Family and there was never any spare money for toys or special activities.

I managed to finish Year 12, although my brother was forced to start working to earn money. I didn't do particularly well in the final years of school and remember those years as tough and unhappy. If you saw me in those days, you'd straightaway think that I was one of many at my school who was going to end up on the dole and not succeed at anything much.

When I finished school I started work in a large bank on a trainee management scheme. I married young and we lived in rental accommodation. We struggled, but I was determined to do well. Soon after we had a baby our marriage ended, which was very distressing for me. Because I had had such a difficult childhood, I was determined that my son would have a better life. I had very little money, but paid child support and other expenses for my departed wife and child.

Some years later I remarried. My new wife had a great deal of faith in me and was extremely supportive. Both of us had come from very poor backgrounds – she had two children from a previous marriage so we were determined to do well for our children. I started getting promotions at work and a company car. We took a risk and borrowed money to buy a house. I went to university and moved through a number of good jobs. An opportunity came up to take on contracting work with a major bank and I decided to set up a company and do it. It was a calculated risk, but I knew that it was the break I had been looking for.

I now have a successful consulting company, nearly own my home and have a number of other investments. I owe my success to a drive to succeed – when someone tells me I can't do something, I really go for it. Coming from a poor background, I would take risks when I saw an opportunity; I always felt I had nothing to lose. My wife has a belief in me that was lacking in my youth. I know I spend too much on the children, holidays and activities, but this is what I missed out on in my childhood and I want to enjoy spending time with my children and ensure they grow up in a happy and vibrant environment. My wife and I know what it is like to have nothing and we're not scared of that. I am a risk taker and it has paid off.

What's your money background?

To change your financial situation you need to examine your own money beliefs and values. Now that you understand what these beliefs and values are, and where they come from, try answering the questions below. They will help you develop a clearer view of your money background and start collecting the support and resources you need. Then use your answers to work out if your inherited values are common sense or if they are holding you back. In other words, give your unconscious beliefs a reality check.

- What were the major incidents in your childhood and teens which influenced the way you view money, saving and finances?
- What influenced your career choices and the way you now plan your financial future?
- What attitudes do you believe have helped you and why?
- Make a list of your financial achievements – for instance, times when you felt that you were spending your money wisely, or through research you got a good bargain, or you managed to save enough money to take a holiday, or you paid off a debt before it was due. What does this tell you? Look for patterns and behaviours that you can build on – for instance, did you make any spending cutbacks to achieve that dream holiday that you could continue to follow every month?
- Similarly, look at the times when your money management may not have worked so well and see if you can work out ways to minimise these times. For instance, do you always find that you're broke at Christmas time, or struggling to pay off the credit card in January?
- Compare situations when managing your money seemed easy and then when it seemed difficult – try to work out what made the difference.
- If you could have someone to help you, what characteristics would they need to have? Do you know anyone who has these characteristics? Do you have any mentors or someone whom you would believe to be a good adviser?
- What resources do you need to help you? Resources aren't just financial; contacts, networks, family and friends are extremely valuable sources of assistance. Make a list of things you can do. For example, meet up with a friend or colleague who may be

able to give you some advice; read books, magazines, newspaper articles, and so on.

The real life stories below illustrate how different our decisions can be depending on the values and beliefs established when we are children. Each person has a very different view of how to manage money. Some were willing to take on the advice of a support team such as accountants and financial planners, while others were extremely reluctant. Many of the decisions they made came consciously or unconsciously from the examples set by their families.

Helen grew up in a home where money was just not discussed, and she now realises how this has affected her own finances.

I grew up as a 'very smart' daughter of a well-respected doctor. In our house discussion of money was not at all encouraged and in fact was considered quite crass. I grew up and went to university and became a doctor like my father. I now realise that although I am capable, I am completely unskilled in relation to anything to do with money. I have spent most of my life avoiding making choices or dealing with money issues at all. I now want to expand my practice and purchase some property and I feel quite fearful about where to start and what to do. This has got a lot to do with my upbringing and our home. I have not helped myself as I have fairly actively avoided learning anything and certainly treat those 'financial advisers' and people who know about money with a great deal of suspicion. Obviously this is silly but it has become a real issue, not just of wanting or feeling motivated to do it but of overcoming my prejudices and the deep-seated values established in my childhood.

Even recently – I went to see a number of accountants. I guess my cynicism about people who know about money was evident at these meetings, as I believed that they couldn't help me. This was reinforced in my mind when they said things like, 'You need a financial planner – I am just an accountant'.

I found it very hard to accept the advice they gave me and as a result I feel somewhat paralysed – I can't see a way of improving my situation.

Ron's childhood experiences have left him with a set of values that are very 'risk averse' – unwilling to take risks. He understands this and has worked out a way to manage around it, by relying on the advice of his financial planner and accountant.

I grew up on a farm in quite impoverished conditions. My father died when we were young and this had a major impact on me. I developed a high level of responsibility and a need to ensure that I financially provided for those I cared for. This has led me to be quite overprotective and conservative in my approach to my finances. I know that there is a risk and reward relationship, but I guess I am just unwilling to do much on the risky side. I am also very careful with my money and try to teach my children this value too. This, I am sure, relates back to my childhood.

I have a financial planner and an accountant who I trust. They have been very influential in helping me work out what decisions to make. If I didn't have them, I think I'd just leave any spare money in the bank, earning virtually no interest. I saw taking out a mortgage as a risk and probably wouldn't have pushed myself to do this without their help. I now own my home and have an investment property. I also have a number of investments that are going very well.

Anita's upbringing gave her the basic ground rules to feel confident making investment decisions.

We grew up in the country and we had a very good life. I understood from a very early age that we were fortunate and I never took this for granted. Dad always emphasised the importance of saving. He always paid cash for things where possible and paid off debts immediately. He hated owing money and believed that we should only spend what we had – not live on borrowings.

I was fortunate to be able to study in America. To do this I took out a loan – I guess this is where I started to really understand saving and rationing or budgeting my money. I was on my own and had to do things myself. When I returned to Australia from the United States, I started thinking seriously about my finances. I talked to as many people as I could find and particularly my dad. I met some 'sharks' as well as a lot of very knowledgeable people who helped me understand things a little. I started reading the newspaper and specialist magazines. Working out how to save money and what to do with it then became like a hobby and a real interest.

I wanted to be able to support myself and have choices. My family had always stressed the importance of being independent and capable of looking after myself.

As you can see it's very important to recognise the lingering effect of your childhood on your financial life now, but this is only the first step. Ron's and Helen's stories show this clearly. Anita was lucky; her family were responsible with money and set a good example. This set her up to study, travel, and value financial independence.

Ron and Brian are doing well too. Ron accepts the advice of his financial planner and accountant, even though it sometimes contradicts what he was brought up to believe was right. Brian has also found a way to overcome the low expectations of his family, and as a result he is now financially secure. Helen, on the other hand, cannot get over the attitudes she learned as a child, and won't accept what the professionals say. Because she is cynical about professional advisers, she finds it hard to choose one she can trust and is left feeling anxious and financially insecure.

It is also important for us to pass on healthy money attitudes to our children. In past generations, money was never talked about, and this is where some of the problems lie. Parents should encourage money conversations with their children. The more we talk to them, the more they understand, and hopefully they'll be better equipped to handle their own finances as they grow older. But don't be surprised when they start questioning where you spend your money!

Money fears

We've discussed how your inherited attitudes to money could be holding you back, making you afraid to take control of your finances. Earlier we mentioned that we had the opportunity to meet a lot of people while promoting our first book. The feedback we received made us realise that many people feel fearful about investing their money. Perhaps their upbringing or a past bad experience led to these fears. Whatever the cause, it is easy to see why many of us haven't started investing.

When we gave our talks about our own experiences of starting an investment club, some of the typical comments we heard from our audiences were about fear and taking that first step. Some were afraid to invest because they were worried about the economy; some didn't start saving because they couldn't decide which type of investment to choose. Some didn't take any risks because they didn't want to get into debt. These concerns all come down to the same thing: fear of losing money. We all feel this way when it comes to our own personal circumstances.

Fear is a very real barrier that you will need to overcome before you start to invest your money. It is through knowledge and under-standing of financial issues that you will be able to release the shackles of your money fears.

After one of our speaking events, a woman approached us and wanted to pass on her reasons why she hadn't been able to take control of her finances. She had always let her husband take care of things and had never been interested in money matters. When they separated she found herself at a loss. For the first time in her life, at sixty years of age, she had to take care of all the bills, banking and other financial issues. She realised that to get on top of her finances, she would have to start educating herself, so she came along to hear our stories.

Our talk helped her to understand that we were like her and everyone else. The only difference is that we were not relying on others to sort out our finances. We wanted to understand and learn for ourselves, so we could be in control. The greater the knowledge you gain, the less fear you have.

Some of our most common fears in relation to money are explored below.

Fear of losing money

You work hard, save your money and the last thing you want is to lose it. This is a reasonable and understandable fear because there is an element of risk involved in becoming financially free. Many millionaires would not have their fortunes if they were risk averse. But even the most experienced investment advisers have made mistakes. The difference between the wealthy and you is that they are prepared to take risks, accept their mistakes, learn from them and move on. Remember, knowledge is power. The more knowledge you have, the better you will cover the risks.

Margaret came along to hear us speak at a *Money Club* breakfast. Here is her story.

I knew I had put my finances on hold for too long, so I decided to go along to hear the girls from The Money Club *speak about their experiences. Little did I know that this would be a turning point for me. I was really inspired and, after listening to their story, I decided I would join an investment club and start investing again. A previous bad experience with a financial adviser had made me very fearful of investing.*

I went through a very bad time financially after my husband left our two year old and me. I eventually got a job and bought a house, and I saw a financial adviser. He said to put my money into superannuation, so I started making contributions. Ten years later I found out that the adviser had opened two separate policies in my name and I was contributing twice the fees.

One fund returned nothing and the other was a low rate of fixed interest. When I found this out I felt betrayed and cheated. As soon as I saw the fees eating into my contributions, I decided to stop the contributions at once. I was scared of losing all my money.

Now I work part-time for a financial institution. Through the confidence I have gained and a boss who is generous with his time and information, I have opened a trading account with an online share trading company. I like being in control again and learning all the jargon, and I did it myself.

Barrier buster

If you're frightened of losing your money in a bad investment, learn how to diversify by spreading your money over different types of investment. In other words, don't put all your eggs into one basket. In Chapter 6 we look at this in more detail.

Fear when money unexpectedly comes your way

This fear is similar to fear of losing your money, and can apply to anyone who has come into a large sum of money, whether it be superannuation, a lump sum payout, an inheritance, a divorce settlement or a lottery win. The problem is, knowing you have money doesn't necessarily take away your fears – and it can make them worse, as you start to worry about what to do with it and how to make sure you don't lose such a large sum through poor investments.

Money management is just as important for people who have a lot of money as those who don't. It would be a tragedy to lose it through lack of financial planning or following the wrong advice. Regardless of the amount of money, large or small, we need to plan wisely and seek the best financial advice to secure the money we have. As always, knowledge is the key to overcoming your fear.

Maxine was in her fifties when her husband died and she came into a large sum of money. She had been out of the workforce for more than thirty years and had left all decisions about money to her husband.

My husband dropped dead of a heart attack with absolutely no warning. The shock was made worse by the fact that I had very little knowledge of financial matters. I was lucky in that my husband had substantial life insurance, but I was worried that this lump sum would have to keep me for the rest of my life. It was a huge responsibility for me to invest this sum wisely, and I was very frightened of making a bad decision and losing my money. I knew there were a lot of shonky investment schemes around and I was determined not to be caught out.

When the insurance money first came through I deposited it with my local bank as a temporary measure. Not surprisingly, the bank was extremely keen for me to invest the money through their in-house financial adviser. I was wary of this, because I knew that I should be looking for a spread of investments, and I wanted an adviser who was independent.

Maxine found her solution by asking around her friends and contacts. She also tested the recommendations they offered to make sure she was comfortable before she committed her money.

A family friend had recently seen a financial planner and I was very impressed that this adviser had advised her to take a superannuation pension, even though the planner would have made a lot more money if she had taken a lump sum instead. Here was an adviser giving independent advice, and not just acting out of self-interest. I went to see the adviser, and the first thing he asked was how much income did I need to live on. From there, he prepared a financial plan that included a wide spread of different types of investments with different institutions. I still have my money invested through this firm. They review my investments every year, and both the value of my capital and my annual income are steadily increasing. It was a huge relief for me to be able to find a firm I could trust. There is no way I could have handled the investment of the insurance proceeds on my own.

Barrier buster

Even if you have a lot of money you still need to manage your finances. Money does not discriminate; you can lose it if you are rich or poor. Hence, money management is important to everyone. With the right information and support, you will feel confident to invest any sum, whether large or small.

Fear of debt

Another fear is that of debt. There are actually two types of debt – good and bad – and all debt is not equal. It's a bit like the good and bad fats in our diet; there are good fats such as extra virgin olive oil, which is monounsaturated, and bad fats such as those found in deep-fried and takeaway foods. We need 'good' fats in our diet to counterbalance the effects of 'bad' fats, which raise our cholesterol levels and clog our arteries. Just as not all fats are bad for you, not all debt is bad for you either.

GOOD DEBT. Good debt is used to buy assets that increase in value. Most Australians would not own their homes if they were afraid of debt. Good debt allows us to achieve our dreams. This is one area where you should leave your fears behind. Just think of the millions of Australians who have taken the plunge and applied for a loan to buy a home. They have both a debt and a growing asset.

Debt can be great way to build wealth, provided it is used to buy assets which increase in value, such as property or shares. Sure, it is riskier than saving up to buy an investment outright. There is a reason though: many wealthy people have successfully used debt to get where they are today.

BAD DEBT. Bad debt is spent on things that won't appreciate in value. Bad debt is borrowing to live beyond your means.

Did you know that your car is a bad debt? The minute you take your new car out of the showroom, its value drops. Compare, say, $30,000 spent on a new car with $30,000 invested in a managed investment fund. Which one will give you a better return over five years? Almost certainly the managed fund.

Yes, most of us need cars and not many people are able to pay cash for a car up-front. This means we borrow money and have to pay the interest charge on top. Understandably so, most people will choose to take on this debt, even if they know it's a bad one. That's fine, as long as you do what you can to minimise bad debt, and at the same time take action to build up assets that will increase in value.

Barrier busters

HOW TO MINIMISE BAD DEBT

1. When looking for a new car, consider buying a car that is one year old. You will still have the benefits of a new car and low kilometres, but you won't have to pay full price.

   For example, the *Glass's Guide to Fleet and Residual Values* estimates that an average Ford Falcon is worth 37% less than its original value after the first year. In the second year and third years, the loss will creep up to 51% off its original value. This is what we mean by a bad debt; it's money spent on an asset that will lose value, so you will never be able to get all your money back when you sell.

2. Once you have a bad debt, pay off your debt as soon as possible. Or, at the very least, stick to your payment plan.

3. If you have a whole lot of small debts with high interest charges, talk to your bank. Apply for a personal loan with a lower interest rate and pay off all the smaller debts using the loan. Have the loan repayments taken directly from your salary every month. If you find yourself with any spare cash, put this money towards the loan. Or you could con-solidate small debts into your home loan and increase your repayments to reduce the debt faster.

4. Plan ahead. Only take on debt if you know you are able to pay it off. It may sound obvious, but it is amazing the number of people who end up with so many debts over a period of time that they have difficulties paying them off.

5. Credit card debt is a classic example of bad debt. See Chapter 5 for some more tips on reducing your credit card debt.

Fear of making wrong choices with money

You are going to make money mistakes. Everyone does. Even the wealthy and the financial experts can make wrong choices. But with careful planning and research, the odds for making wrong decisions will be greatly narrowed. So your aim should be to get it right most of the time.

The trick is to cut down on the number of mistakes and the severity of their consequences. The smartest money managers in the world occasionally get it wrong. What makes them so smart is that even when they do get it wrong, it is not a financial disaster for them. They have protected themselves, and you can learn how to do this as well.

Look back to Ron's story. His father died when Ron was young, and the family were impoverished. Naturally, Ron grew up to be very conservative with money, and frightened of taking risks. Yet he managed to overcome his fear, by finding advisers he could trust and learning about the relationship between risk and reward.

Barrier busters

1. Instead of worrying, start the learning process. Remember, knowledge is the key. Armed with knowledge you will be able tackle your fears head on.

2. Read, listen, ask questions and learn.

3. In most capital cities, the Australian Stock Exchange runs some terrific investor education programs. The 'Investor Hour' at lunchtime only costs $5 (at the time of writing) and is a great opportunity to hear people who work in the finance industry discuss their particular field of expertise. You can log onto the Australian Stock Exchange website for more information (www.asx.com.au) or phone 1300 300 279.

4. Talk to your friends and get some practical advice from your peers. If all else fails, start learning together, as we did in our investment club.

5. Make time to see a financial adviser and ask questions. Ask as many questions as you need to feel comfortable before you make any commitment. Most of the major banks have a financial adviser. This is a good place to start even though they may be pushing their own investment products. If you are a long-standing customer of the bank then they should willingly offer the services of one of their financial advisers.

Some people can't or won't make financial decisions; they are paralysed with fear. Even though doing nothing might feel like a safe option, it is probably costing them dearly in lost opportunities. Doing nothing is a decision in itself, and not a very good one. One way to overcome this type of fear is to find out more about what scares you; another is to find the right sort of professional help, as Maxine and Ron did.

Lack of time

It is easy to understand why lack of time is the number one hurdle for many people. Today we are expected to juggle many tasks, from holding down a job or study to running a household and making time for our children and partners. It's no wonder we put off sorting through our finances for another day or another time.

But somehow we all need to find the time. Even starting with as little as half an hour a week will really help. You may say, 'I don't have a spare half hour', but just think of the things you regularly do in a half hour; watch your favourite sitcom; take a lunch break or have coffee with a friend. You may have to trade off one of these favourite activities once a week to begin with, but just remember, the time you put aside to organise your finances will be time well spent.

Everyone is in the same boat. Before we started our investment club, we all had pretty much the same excuses: 'I don't have time', 'I work long hours' or 'I'm too tired after working and looking after the kids to think about money'. Even so, we all had an underlying determination to do something with our finances, and that's why an investment club really worked for us. It became a forum for discussion on the topic of investment and helped us make time to learn together.

Take a look at your colleagues and friends, particularly those you regard as good money managers. Their time is just as precious. The difference is that they had the *desire* to take control of their finances. Perhaps in some cases they were forced to through their personal circumstances.

It's important to understand that the road to becoming financially fit doesn't happen overnight, so don't panic when you don't instantly have things the way you want them. Think of it this way: you wouldn't turn up to the starting line of a marathon without training. If you did, you'd only run a couple of kilometres before you'd give it up and say it's too hard. When training for a marathon, you need to begin with short sessions, gradually building up mileage and confidence along the way. The same applies to learning to become financially fit. Just start with small steps and little by little, your confidence and your ability will grow, until suddenly the previously impossible seems easy.

Why you shouldn't put it off for another day

If you've been putting off looking at your finances, you may find that events suddenly force you to, whether you're ready or not – for example, marriage, divorce, retrenchment or retirement. At some point in your life you will be faced with at least one or more of these situations.

Becoming financially fit is a life's journey – it's never too late to get started.

If you continually use the 'lack of time' excuse, think about this. Picture yourself some 10 to 20 years in the future. Like many people, you have continued to live your life without savings. You are still renting and the job prospects for people over 50 years old are somewhat precarious. Is this where you want to be?

Now think back to all the hours you have invested into your career, sport, marriage or relationship to reap the benefits. So too there will be rewards for investing the time to take control of your finances.

How do we find the time?

Frances, Emily, Di and Dianne all work and have children. Here's an example of how Emily and Dianne manage to find time in their weekly routine to keep up with their finances.

EMILY. *I find the best time for me to catch up on the financial news is straight after my morning walk. I make sure I drop into my local cafe, which has all the daily papers. I check the shares and read other relevant news. I meet a number of other locals at our cafe and* *sometimes we even talk about our shares. I really enjoy this part of the day.*

DIANNE. *My daughter has a dancing lesson every Monday after school. While I wait for her to finish, I grab a coffee and read through the financial magazines. I also save any other articles I want to read for this time. I know I have to wait 45 minutes for her to finish, so I might as well use this time wisely.*

Think about what time you can set aside each week. Start talking to your friends, especially if they are as keen as yourself. You can learn together and enjoy the whole process, as we did. Once you begin to understand the language of 'investing', it will start to become second nature.

We all work and have families, so we understand that it's easy to forget or make excuses to leave it for another time. But what we have learnt from our own experiences and that of others is that you need to take responsibility for your financial future. Don't wait until one of life's unexpected events, such as retrenchment or divorce, throws you in at the deep end.

Barrier busters

1. Start by reading the business pages of the newspapers during a morning break. If you find this too daunting, then try reading the 'Money' supplements which most of the main newspapers carry, usually once a week. In general, they are easier to read and targeted to non-financial readers. They also cover many topics, from superannuation to retirement, and there is always a financial adviser column, where readers ask for advice.
2. Each weekday morning, you'll hear reports about the stock market and general business news on your local TV and radio. Get into the habit of listening to these reports before you set off for the day. Radio is great for accessing information while you're on the go.

Managing your time

Look at your big picture. When you feel overwhelmed from too much to do, as we all do from time to time, make a list of everything you need to do and prioritise. What is the most important thing you need to do right now? Do you have a plan for each day with your priority jobs listed for action? An easy way is to write down your jobs in order of priority on a 'to do' list. Or write them straight into your diary. You'll find once you get into the habit of tackling the priority jobs first, you will feel a sense of achievement.

Sue has a busy life like us – here's how she does it!

MORNING. *I'm more of a morning person, so I find the best time for me to organise the day ahead is to take time out in the morning. I get up between 6 and 6.30 am. Hopefully the kids are still in bed.*

I begin the day with my morning walk (going to the gym would just take up too much time) and reading the papers. By the time I'm back from my walk, the kids are up and we begin the process of getting everyone ready for school and work. All of this has to be done before I get out the door!

By 9 am I am at the office. My first priorities are to make important phone calls and reply to my emails. Then I look at my diary to see what tasks I need to complete that day.

LUNCHTIME. *I usually pay bills at lunchtime and I do this over the phone or via the internet. (In today's world, if there is any positive about paying bills, it's that you can do it anytime, weekend, day or night.)*

I also check the share prices on the internet.

EVENING. *This is a particularly frenetic time in my household, because my husband and I both work. I go through the mail, start dinner and settle the children, but my main priority is to help the children with their homework.*

Time management is really a question of juggling priorities. There are so many legitimate demands on our time, especially if you have a very demanding job, or children, or both, as we do. You might feel that sorting out your finances is an exceptionally time-consuming task. The trick is to set up a system that is relatively low maintenance once it is up and running. For example, if Sue went to the gym in the morning, this would add an extra half hour of travelling time. By walking straight out the door for her morning walk she can use this half hour to catch up on the financial news. Another added benefit is that walking is free, so saves on gym fees.

Barrier busters

1. Write down everything you do in one day. Can you see where time could have been saved? If one day is not enough, do a week's schedule. You will need to establish how you can save time, along with identifying the time-wasters.

2. Don't underestimate the time involved in running a household, particularly if you have children. If the children are old enough, give them chores. Explain to them how valuable their help is to you. Give them rewards for helping.

3. If your children are still young and they can't help with the household cleaning, it may pay to hire a cleaner if you can afford to. It's difficult for anyone to come home from work and have to spend time cleaning the house. Time is a valuable commodity, and it might be better spent helping your children with homework or sorting through your own paperwork.

4. Take some reading material with you while you wait for appointments, such as at the doctor and hairdresser, or on train and bus trips into work. In general, once you start to take more of an interest in your finances, reading related topics will become easier and more interesting and you'll be more inclined to fit it into your daily routine.

5. Spend a few minutes a day sorting through your bills. Have a folder for credit card bills only; stick your credit card receipts onto a piece of paper and mark off every item once you receive your credit card statement.

6. Use your diary effectively. Disorganised people may have a diary, but they don't have the habit of writing in it and checking their schedule each day.

7. Use the internet for banking and paying your bills. Telephone banking is another alternative. The main advantage of electronic payment methods is to cut down your travel time and the time you have to wait in queues. Whenever you can, opt to have bills paid automatically from a nominated account or credit card.

8. Set aside some time to organise a filing system for your financial records. We find late Sunday afternoon the best time in our busy schedules for sorting out finances. It still allows time with family and does not impinge too much on the weekend.

9. If you can't face doing your tax return, pay a tax agent or accountant to do it. This is a tax-deductible cost.

10. Once your tax return is done, file the documents away in a safe place for the next six years, and then destroy them. The Tax Office only asks you keep records for the past six years.

11. Try not to let the paperwork build up. If the pile gets too big, it becomes daunting and time-consuming, and then the vicious cycle of procrastination kicks in. Organisation is the key. Once you have taken the time initially to set up folders, you can file paperwork as soon as it comes in or as soon as a bill is paid. This will alleviate the burden when it comes to finding your bills, statements or any paperwork. You won't be rummaging through piles of paper and wasting time.

12. Investment clubs are a great time-saver. You save time by sharing the load and gathering information between club members. Our book *The Money Club* helped many others who were like us and needed the kick-start.

13. Visit your local library or bookstore. There are dozens of easy to read self-help books on time management. Our recommendation is *The 7 Habits of Highly Effective People*, by Stephen Covey.

14. Try searching the web to find a time management course. There are hundreds across Australia and generally they are very affordable. The Australian Institute of Management runs such a course in every state – phone 1300 651 811.

CHAPTER 2

Goal setting and planning

All children dream about the future, about the wonderful life they will live when they finally grow up. When the time comes, and at last we are adults, it's easy to lose sight of our dreams. We get caught up in our day-to-day dramas at work and at home. Now that we are going to look at our life goals, it's time to go back and do a little more dreaming. How long is it since you really thought about what makes you happy, about the sort of life you want to live?

Setting your life goals goes hand in hand with planning your finances. If you haven't thought about your life goals, how will you know if your financial plan is going to help you get there? We all want to be happy, and we know that money alone can't buy happiness. Money can give you choices, and it can give you the time you need to really go after what you want to do. When we plan our finances, it's not really about money; it's about what sort of life we want to be living.

What are your dreams? What do you need to do to make them happen? Financial freedom is about having control over your money and therefore more choices in your life. You can choose to change to a more interesting or fulfilling job; to take time off work to travel or study; to spend time with your children; or to pursue whatever you are passionate about. These are the rewards of financial fitness.

It's easy to get caught up in a cycle of needing, or wanting, more and more money. Sometimes we think, 'Oh, if only I had enough money to pay off the mortgage, have security in retirement, a good education for the kids, an overseas holiday . . .' It feels as though our finances can never catch up with our lifestyles. Dreaming of being very rich can leave us vulnerable to investment scams (see Chapter 11 for more details) that trade on our fantasies of becoming fabulously wealthy without having to work hard. There's nothing wrong with wanting to be extremely rich (we would all like to win the lottery), but do you have a realistic plan to achieve this? If not, and to be honest most of us don't, setting life goals you know you can achieve will put you in control and ultimately lead to a much greater sense of satisfaction.

Embarking on any journey requires change. You might have already started your journey, and reading this book is part of that process. Or you might want to change, but are looking for a trigger, or catalyst, to make change happen. Look back at times you've changed in the past – was it always as a response to things that happened to you, or did you initiate the change yourself?

For example, have you ever tried to change the way you look through exercise? Some people embark on a physical fitness program with vague goals: 'I want to feel fit and healthy' or 'I want to look more toned'. Life or financial goals can be just as vague: 'I don't want to have to worry about money' or 'I want to have enough super'. Doesn't it seem more effective to work towards a specific goal, such as 'I want to lose two kilos' or 'I want to retire when I'm 55 with an annual income of $40,000'?

Most of us devote a large proportion of our time and energy to working towards our business or career goals. We may have projects or action plans that aim to deliver a result to the organisation we work for. Why don't we put the same amount of time into doing this exercise at home – for our own life goals, plans and strategies?

When large organisations hire consultants to coach their managers in leadership and planning skills, this type of business coaching will usually include sessions on personal planning and setting life goals. The people doing the course often resist the personal planning sessions at first; like the rest of us, they have never really sat down and planned their personal goals before. This could be due to lack of time, or not putting a high priority on their personal goals, but often it can simply be that the managers just don't know how to go about it.

Like sporting coaches, who devise regular training programs for athletes to help them achieve their goals, life coaches help their clients achieve their life goals, in their careers or relationships. A life coach might start by asking you to write down your short, medium and long-term goals.

Next, a life coach will help you work out a weekly or monthly plan to help you achieve your goals. This means breaking down what you must do to achieve the goals into small manageable steps, so you can start putting the plan into action right away. Then, every week or month, you check in with your life coach and report back on your progress. Just as a personal trainer will drag you out of bed at 6 am to exercise, a life coach will force you to actually translate your plans into action.

Lots of us resist planning for the things we really want. It can be difficult and we can find a million reasons not to do it today. Anyone can develop their life plan; it doesn't require any particular skills. All you need is a piece of paper, a pen, and an hour or so of uninterrupted time. To get you started on this process, here's a quick rundown of the issues you can look at to get your own life plan in place.

1. Define your goals

See what short, medium and long-term goals you can come up with.

- **Short-term goals (up to 12 months)**
  For example: paying off your credit card debt; saving for travel or a deposit on a house or flat; renovating or redecorating if you already have your own home.
- **Medium-term goals (one to three years)**
  For example: taking a course to improve your qualifications or

just learn more about something that interests you; travelling; going for a promotion at work or a better job.

- **Long-term goals (over three years)**
  For example: moving to a larger or smaller place, depending on your family needs; more extensive travel; maybe a career change or becoming self-employed.

It can be hard to set long-term goals when you're young. The future seems a long way off, and who knows how things will turn out. You don't necessarily have to have your retirement all mapped out when you are in your twenties, but having, say, a ten-year plan is a good idea, to work against the temptation to just live for the moment, from pay to pay. Setting long-term goals doesn't have to be limiting – people modify their goals all the time.

Although goal setting involves some delayed gratification (why can't I just have everything now?), you can and should build in some fun things; for example, an overseas holiday every few years, or taking time off from work to do whatever it is you love. It's easier, and more meaningful, to put in an effort now if you have a worthwhile longer-term goal to work towards.

2. Work out your 'Money Picture'

What's your financial snapshot right now? This is what we have called your 'Money Picture'. Are you getting ahead or falling behind? You need to work out where you are now before you can move ahead. The next chapter will take you through a financial Health Check so you can build up a 'Money Picture' of your current situation.

3. Set your plan

Using your goals and Money Picture, set your plan. How much money do you need to save in the short, medium and long term to achieve your goals? How are you going to build wealth? What can you afford to buy now, and what will have to wait until next year, or later?

4. Take action

It's all very well to have short and long-term goals, an analysis of strengths and weaknesses, and all the self-knowledge in the world – you still need to put together a workable strategy to implement it all.

The key to implementing your goals is to break down tasks into small manageable items, which can be achieved and ticked off every week. This ties in well with most time management strategies, which also concentrate on breaking up seemingly huge and over-whelming tasks into smaller, manageable chunks. For example, your short-term goal might be to have a great Christmas. To do this, you'll need to start putting aside money now. The steps you might take could look like this:

GOAL PLANNING SHEET

My goal
To save $1,000 for next Christmas.

Benefits of achieving this goal
To have enough money so that I can buy presents and have some fun without worrying whether I can afford it.

Specific action steps to achieve this goal
1. Work out how much I need to save each month to reach my goal.
2. Research savings accounts to find the one with the lowest fees and highest interest (www.aca.com.au has comparisons).
3. Open the account.
4. Contact the pay office at work to arrange for the money to be directly transferred to the new account every month.
5. Hide or destroy the chequebook or card attached to the account so I can't take any money out before Christmas.

Here are a few more tips on how to implement your plan and achieve your goals.

Barrier busters

1. Write in your diary the tasks you have set yourself for the week or the month, such as opening the Christmas account, or making sure that you pay your credit card off by the due date. Tick them off once completed. Don't forget to look in the diary regularly!
2. If you don't keep a diary, or don't trust yourself to look at it regularly, put your list somewhere obvious, such as on the fridge door, so you can't let yourself forget about it.
3. Collaborate with a close friend, relative or colleague, without necessarily revealing to each other every detail of what is in your plan. Encourage each other; it's like having a fitness buddy to make you get out of bed to go for a walk in the morning.
4. Reward yourself along the way. What relatively inexpensive activity gives you the most pleasure? It could be seeing a movie, subscribing to your favourite magazine, following or playing sport. Whatever it is, include it in your plan and make sure to do it regularly. Planning does not mean putting off everything you enjoy for the future.
5. Be positive. Believe that you will achieve your goals. There is nothing like positive affirmation to get you where you want to be.

From time to time you might feel as though you're not making much progress, that your goals are too ambitious, or too far off in the future. Don't use such setbacks as an excuse to abandon your plan completely. Reviewing your goals and assessing your progress in achieving them is a continuous process. Think about the goals you have successfully achieved so far. Quite possibly there was a time when you never thought you'd make it, but looking back now you can see that perseverance has paid off. Keep that sense of confidence and achievement and don't lose sight of your life goals; they are the big picture, the motivation and reward for all your planning.

CHAPTER 3

Health Check – testing your financial fitness

Right, crunch time. You have examined your attitudes and fears, and how you can make time to set your goals and look after your financial fitness. Now it's time to take an honest look at your finances. Do you know where all your hard-earned dollars have gone? How well do you really manage your money?

When you go for a medical heath check you will probably be asked to complete a form with a number of questions about your health, which you answer honestly so that the practitioner can help you. Assessing the state of your finances is a similar process. Taking a financial health check will give you a clear picture of where you are. Unless you have that in front of you, you won't be able to make your own diagnosis and consider the realistic actions and options you can take to recover, build and secure your finances. Now that's got to be worth spending a bit of your time on.

If you have a black hole in your wallet or purse then start with the Cash Diary. The next step is to build your personal Money Picture so you can see where your money comes from and where it goes. Even if you think you are managing your money well, you might get a shock when you sit down to do your Health Check and see what colour result you get. Will you be Red, Amber or Green?

Keep a 'Cash Diary'

The Cash Diary is the starting point for those of us who regularly withdraw cash from the ATM and then say, 'Where has it all gone?'. By using our Cash Diary, you will now know the answer. Don't be put off, as this is not as big a job as it seems.

For one week only, record every item you spend using cash. Then write it down in your diary.

Here is an example you can use for your cash diary. If you don't have time for a week, do one day and then make an estimate for the week, or as a minimum spend 10 minutes now and do an estimate of your weekly cash spending.

MY CASH DIARY FOR THE WEEK OF .... TOTAL SPENT $.........

What I spent	Monday	Tuesday	Wednesday	Thursday	Friday	Saturday	Sunday
Bus pass	$15						
Drinks, lunch and snacks	$10.10						
Magazine	$4.90						
Bottle of wine	$15						
TOTAL	$45						

From your receipts on Monday you could find that you have spent:

- $15 on a bus pass
- $1.50 on an orange juice on the way to work
- $2 on a mid-morning coffee
- $4.60 on a takeaway sandwich at lunch
- $4.90 on a magazine
- $2 on a chocolate bar in the afternoon, plus
- $15 on a bottle of wine bought on the way home

Even though each one of these items doesn't seem a large amount, when you add up the total for the day, it's $45. If you spend a similar amount every day and multiply this day's total across seven days, you have spent $315 dollars.

Barrier buster

Always ask for a receipt, so you have a true record of your spending. Put all the receipts in an envelope, a plastic folder sleeve or a tray, or on a spike – whatever, just make sure you collect them.

Build your 'Money Picture'

Now that you have completed your Cash Diary for a week, or made an estimate, we can move onto building your Money Picture. It simply shows you a clear and complete picture of where your money comes from and, more importantly, where it goes. Once you complete your Money Picture, then our Health Check will assess your current state of financial fitness.

You will need records such as your bank statements, pay slips, chequebook and credit card statements and any other records you have of your expenses over the last month. Now you need to set aside a couple of hours, relax, put some music on, grab a drink and let's get started.

Our template, which follows, is an example of how you can record the information to build your Money Picture. First, transfer the expenses from your Cash Diary into the first column, 'Weekly cash', next to the appropriate category. Multiply this amount by 52 weeks and put the yearly figure in the third column, 'Estimated 12 months'.

For example, if you spend a total of $20 each week on lunch and coffees then transfer this amount into the first column. Then multiply by 52, which equals $1,040, and put this amount in column three, 'Estimated 12 months'.

Now go through your credit card statements, bank statements and any other records you have, and put down exactly where your money is being spent. Convert all your expenses into an annual figure. Weekly expenses such as lunches should be multiplied by 52, and monthly expenses such as the phone bill should be multiplied by 12. Some expenses are likely to be a one-off occurrence, such as a holiday or insurance. Put these amounts into the 'Estimated 12 months' column.

The categories in the table are expenditure suggestions from us, but only you know the real picture. For you to take an honest picture of where your money goes, you need to break it down as much as possible to match the types of expenses you have.

MY MONEY PICTURE: EXPENSES

	Weekly cash	This month	Estimated 12 months	Total
HOUSEHOLD				
Rent/mortgage				
Council rates				
Electricity/gas				
Strata levies				
Water rates				
Cleaning/maintenance				
Repairs				
Home/contents insurance				
Other?				
TOTAL				$............
FAMILY/CHILDREN/EDUCATION				
Childcare costs				
School fees/other expenses for the children, e.g. pocket money				
Courses/seminars				
Other?				
TOTAL				$............
MEDICAL/HEALTH AND SPORT				
Medical (doctor/chemist/dentist – deduct any medical fund rebates)				
Fitness/gym/treatments				
Health insurance				
Other?				
TOTAL				$............

	Weekly cash	This month	Estimated 12 months	Total
ENTERTAINMENT				
Videos/DVDs				
Going out (movies, clubs, etc)				
Other?				
TOTAL				$...........
FOOD AND EATING OUT				
Food/groceries				
Alcohol				
Going out to eat/takeaway food				
Lunch and coffees at work	$20		$1,040	
Other?				
TOTAL				$...........
CLOTHES AND PERSONAL ITEMS				
Clothes and shoes				
Hair/personal products/beauty				
Dry cleaning				
Other?				
TOTAL				$...........
LIFESTYLE AND INDULGENCES				
Cigarettes				
Holidays				
Gifts/pressies				
Other?				
TOTAL				$...........
TELECOMMUNICATIONS				
Telephone/mobile phone				
Internet service provider				
Other?				
TOTAL				$...........
TRAVEL				
Transport (bus, train, taxis, etc)				
Motor vehicle (loan repayments, lease, petrol, cleaning, registration, insurance, maintenance and repairs)				
Other?				
TOTAL				$...........

	Weekly cash	This month	Estimated 12 months	Total
FINANCIAL				
Bank fees and government charges				
Bank interest/credit card interest				
Donations				
Life insurance				
Credit card (or other) loan repayment				
Advisers (accountant, financial planner, lawyer)				
Other?				
TOTAL				$...........
A. TOTAL	$...........	$............	$.............	$...........

Now let's turn to where your money comes from. This is usually much easier to do than expenses because most of us only have a few sources of income. Put down for the same month as your expenses above the income received. If you are paid weekly then multiply by 52 weeks divided by 12 months. If you are paid fortnightly then multiply by 26 weeks divided by 12 months.

MY MONEY PICTURE: INCOME

	This month*	This year
Net salary/commission		
Bonus		
Interest income from savings or investments		
Rental income		
Dividend income from shares		
Unit trust distributions		
Money owed to you and being repaid		
Tax return refund		
Other		
B. TOTAL	$.............	$.............

*the same month in which you have completed the cash diary and recorded your expenses

Before you move on to the Health Check:

1. Have you covered all the areas where you spend your money? Make one last check.
2. Are there any other sources from which you receive money?
3. Total your spending and income for the year.

Now it's time to use the figures from your Money Picture to make a Health Check diagnosis. We have used those familiar traffic light colours: Red, Amber and Green. Red, of course means *Stop*. Amber means *Caution*. Green means *GO* and should be your eventual goal.

Your 'Health Check'

Take the total yearly figures from your Money Picture and insert into the Health Check sheet.

MY HEALTH CHECK

FROM YOUR MONEY PICTURE	RESULT OF YOUR FITNESS TEST
A. Total money out $	*If C is **negative**, you are RED.*
B. Total money in $	*If C is **zero**, you are ORANGE.*
C. B minus A $	*If C is **positive**, you are GREEN.*

Now read the section below that applies to you.

Red means STOP!

If you are Red, you have more money going out than coming in. This is not a sustainable position for anyone who wants to be financially fit. Don't panic, there are a number of things you can do in the short term to improve your position. Your Health Check indicates that your priority is to go on a Money Diet. This means looking at where you can reduce your spending and use that money to start paying off any debts you have.

We help you plan your Money Diet in the next chapter and work with you on what actions you need to take. It's not realistic to expect that you will be in a position to start saving while you're in the Red. The goal here is to recover. For instance, if you have a credit card debt charging interest at 17%, you need to concentrate on paying it off, rather than opening a savings account which might only pay 3% interest. It is only when you reach Amber that you can begin to save. Remember, we talked about breaking up the 'big picture' into small achievable steps. Prioritising where you spend your money is one of those steps. Like any diet, you will also need to take action to break any bad money habits you have developed which put your Health Check in Red. Chapter 5 looks at breaking bad habits. These could be overspending, credit card debt or addictions. You are not alone; bad habits can affect us all, regardless of whether we are Green, Amber or Red. The difference for you in Red is that you need to take action now, as you have no money buffer.

If you are Red, go to

Chapter 4 for your Money Diet
Chapter 5 for how to break those bad money habits

Amber means CAUTION

If you are Amber, while you're *not* in the red now, you need to take action to make sure you don't slip into Red. You cannot stay in Amber if your aim is to be financially fit. What are your goals? Did you write them down from Chapter 2? Your goals need to be set before you can start planning on how to move into Green. They will give you the gift of motivation to start saving. To save you must reduce your current expenses, or increase your income. How can you do this? You can succeed by planning your Money Diet in the next chapter, working out what actions you will take, and then sticking to them.

If you are Amber, go to

Chapter 2 to write down your life goals and plans
Chapter 4 for your Money Diet
Chapter 5 for how to break those bad money habits

Green means GO

Congratulations! If the result of your Health Check is Green, this means a clean bill of health.

Your hard work has paid off and you are firmly on track to financial freedom. The trick is to maintain your fitness. Your next step is to secure your position by building your wealth so that it earns money for you. Start off by having a look at your Money Diet, as there may still be some places where you can reduce the money going out and have even more to save. Then it's time for learning the basics on investing in Chapter 6 and making decisions on how and where to put your money to build your wealth. Then move onto Chapter 7, where we show you how others have built their wealth. Merely putting your money in the bank is not the way to achieve this. You can do a stocktake of your wealth picture now and where you want to go using the goals you set in Chapter 2.

If you are GREEN, go to

Chapter 2 to write down your life goals and plans
Chapter 4 for your Money Diet
Chapter 5 for how to get rid of any lingering bad habits
Chapter 6 for investing to learn the basics and then make decisions on how and where to put your money
Chapter 7 for building your wealth

The Health Check is an important step in your financial fitness program. The next step, using the results of your Health Check, is to plan your Money Diet and decide what actions you can take to achieve it. Rather than having that usual 'out of control feeling' when thinking about your finances, taking action means taking control and feeling good about it, just like going on a diet and then fitting into those jeans you've wanted to be able to wear for ages.

CHAPTER 4

Planning your Money Diet

What was your Health Check result? Are you Red, with more money going out than coming in, Amber, just breaking even by spending all the money you have coming in, or Green, with more coming in than going out? Like any fitness test, your financial Health Check results will change over time. What never changes is the Money Cycle; how much money is coming in, how much is going out, and how much is left.

Using the Money Picture, which looks at what has happened in the past, you can plan your Money Diet, starting with the Money Cycle, your cashflow in any given month. What amount of money will you have at the beginning of the month – most likely the amount that's in your bank account or cash management account? Add to this the amount you expect to get in that month (let's say your pay) and then work out an estimate of the money that will go out (your Money Picture will help with this estimate). The end of the cycle is what's left and is the starting point for the next month. Is this how much you need? Is the money going out where you want it to go? What decisions do you need to make? What Diet Plan do you need and what steps can you take to stick to it?

MY MONEY CYCLE

A. Money at start of the month	Bank account	$	
	Cash management account	$	
	Other	$	
	TOTAL		$..............
B. Money in during the month	Salary	$	
	Interest income	$	
	Other (dividends/rent)	$	
	TOTAL		$..............
ADD A and B			$..............
C. Money out	*Fixed* These are the things that *have* to be paid, such as rent, car repayments, loan repayment, credit card payment, insurance	$	
	Discretionary These are the things that you don't have to spend money on or can choose how much you spend, such as clothes, grooming, hair, make-up, magazines, food and entertainment	$	
	Wealth building This is where you are putting your money into assets such as superannuation, managed investments, or your mortgage. If you have put some of these under fixed, move them here because the money is going into assets which are wealth building.	$	
	TOTAL		$..............
TOTAL	A plus B less C = money left at the end of the month		$..............

Now you have a complete picture of money coming in and money going out. What is your Diet Plan? What decisions and actions are you going to take? Well, let's have a look at each area.

Increasing the money coming in

One of the things you might consider as part of your Diet Plan is how to increase the money coming in. If you were Red in your Health Check, this may not be a choice but a necessity. Perhaps you are Amber and want to move to Green and start building your wealth. There are several options for increasing your income.

1. Make more money in your current job

This is the action that most people think of last but it should be your first port of call. Don't assume your company will automatically pay 'what you are worth.' First, get together some facts about how much other people are being paid to do your job in similar organisations. Don't know? Then make an appointment with a recruitment firm who recruits in your industry. Take a copy of your position description, or if you don't have one, write a list of your responsibilities and role. Log on to the internet to recruitment and job sites to establish what the market rate is for the job you are currently doing.

Is this what you are being paid? No? Then the next step is set up a meeting with your boss or whoever the most appropriate person is (perhaps someone from the human resources area), to assess the value of your role and then make a decision or recommendation on your salary. Tell them what the meeting is about so they can come prepared. In your meeting set out your facts, don't personalise the issue, and most importantly don't threaten (*If I don't get a pay rise then I'll resign!*). After setting out the facts, allow your boss to comment, and give him or her time to come back to you with a response. Make sure you agree on a date for this. Once you have your response then you will know the next step to take. In the meantime, it is always a good idea to keep your résumé or CV (curriculum vitae) current and to keep learning new skills that will add to your 'value'.

2. Get a new job

Do a stocktake of your marketable skills. Review the list. Is there an area where you need to increase your marketability and therefore your chances? If so, check out ways to gain these skills, such as through courses or training. Also, to improve your chances of getting the job and salary you want, invest some time and money into preparing your résumé or CV. There are companies who deal specifically in preparing CVs and you can find them in the job section of the newspaper or on the internet.

Once you have your CV, make an appointment with a recruitment company in your field, look on the internet and in the job section of the newspapers. Also, use the network you have to get an introduction. Talk to people and then talk more.

3. Take on a second job

When considering this option you need to assess how much time you have and what would suit you best for a second job. Would having a second job have an impact on your full-time job, or your family or relationship? Perhaps you could put an ad in the paper and use your day job skills to do work at home? What about starting a business and building it up while still getting the pay from your day job, until you are in a position to work in the business full-time?

4. Other ways to increase your income

What other ways can you make more money? This is where you can be creative. It could be as simple as renting out a spare room or garage, renting out your house while you're on holidays, having a garage sale or selling your old clothes to a recycling shop. Go through all your assets – is there anything you don't use which would be of value to someone else? Go to the *Trading Post* website or ring up the local paper and see how much it costs to put in an ad. An investment of 15 minutes of your time could make a difference to your financial fitness – every bit helps.

Reducing the money going out on areas which don't build your wealth

The money out section of your Diet Plan can be divided into three categories. First are the fixed expenses – these are the expenses we rank as being totally necessary, such as paying the rent, essential bills and loan repayments. Next are discretionary expenses. These are expenses that we have choices about, so will be the main area we can focus on to cut down our expenditure. This will require you to look closely at each expense, and work out which discretionary expenses are important and which are a waste of money. Then finally the best category: the wealth building, where our money is going out but going into an area that is working for us by producing an income and/or a capital gain.

Money out – fixed

Even with fixed costs there are things you can do to reduce the money going out. Do you have a number of loans, such as credit cards or personal loans? Can you reduce the amount you pay on interest and charges? Talk to your bank, and look up some internet sites such as www.choice.com.au for help. Yes, you need to invest some time doing this research, but it's worth it to see how much you can save. To give another example, have you checked out your mortgage repayments? How much interest are you paying? Can you get a cheaper rate from your bank, or another bank or through a mortgage broker?

When you are doing these investigations don't forgot to also ask how much it will cost you to 'switch' from one loan to another. To find out how much you'll save over the life of the loan, your new lender will be more than happy to do the calculation for you. You can also use the calculators on any of the major banks' websites.

Let's take another example of 'fixed' expenses – car repayments. You must have a car – right? Perhaps you could look at how much it is really costing you each year. Add up all the expenses from this category in your Money Picture. Have you investigated what the cost might be to take taxis or use public transport instead? Does your household have two cars? If so, can you sell one and work out a way to share the other? Can you trade in your car for a smaller one that costs less to run? These aren't easy decisions but they could result in substantial savings.

Money out – discretionary

In your Health Check in Chapter 3, as part of working out your Money Picture, you listed all your expenses, or money out. You can now use this list to make some decisions about where you can reduce the money going out. The aim here is to work out where you can cut back without having to make drastic changes to your current lifestyle. This is where your Money Diet goes into action. Go through and rank all your outgoings in order of priority – number your expenses with number one being a necessity and the highest number being your lowest priority. What outgoings can you choose to make a lower priority to achieve your financial goal, be it saving for a holiday or car, or to start investing? This is how you use your Money Picture and Money Cycle – they are your tools to take control of the money that goes out every month.

Let's say you're in Red with a $1,000 credit card debt that you want to pay off. Using your Health Check and Money Diet, here's how you can get out of it.

MY MONEY DIET

1. Health Check	Do my Money Picture and see the result of my Health Check. Result: I'm Red and need to plan an immediate Money Diet and find out where my money is going.
2. What is my goal?	Recover my position and move into Amber – my first goal is to pay off my credit card debt of $1,000 in 10 weeks
3. Money Diet actions I will take to achieve my goal	1. Take lunch to work each day = save $30 per week. 2. Don't go out for dinner once per week = save $40 (Invite my friends over for dinner instead, everyone brings a plate of food and bottle of wine and we have a great night in!) 3. Reduce my mobile calls by $10 per week 4. Don't use a taxi – take the bus or walk = $10 per week 5. Cut down two takeaway coffees per day to one = $10 per week This adds up to $100 per week, that I can pay straight to the bank to pay off my debt. 6. Take my credit card out of my wallet and leave it at home (or destroy it) and pay cash for anything I buy.
4. Result	With $400 a month paid off my credit card debt, within three months I'm debt free and in Amber. It wasn't as hard as I thought. My next goal is to start to save – and to do that I need to plan another Money Diet.

Spending less

How to spend less is the eternal question, and you now have the answer by unlocking the past through your Money Picture and looking at the present in your Money Cycle, and planning your Money Diet for the future. Here are some diet tips that have worked for others and us in saving money.

The key thing to think about is how much value you get out of each dollar spent. The obvious items to get rid of are the low priority, low visibility items that don't do anything for you. This could be reducing your bank fees or the interest you pay as a result of not paying your credit cards off on time. Also, we all from time to time fall into false economies such as not getting the car serviced and then having major repairs, or buying some clothes on sale that don't fit and then never wearing them.

Often the things you spend unnecessary money on are a time–money tradeoff. For example, you didn't get time to go to the supermarket so you will buy takeaway dinner instead. Taxis are another good example of this – usually there is another way to get where you are going. Take some time to go through our Money Diet tips and see which ones might also work for you.

Money Diet tips

How much does it cost you to run your household – your insurance, car, phones, transport to and from work, clothing yourself and the family, educating yourself and family, and keeping fit and healthy? Here are our tried and true diet tips for where you can cut back on the money going out.

Household
- What things do you buy for the house that you don't really need? Can you sell anything that you bought and don't use anymore? What's in the garage that you don't use?
- Before paying $80 for a service repair call, decide whether it is likely the washing machine or video player is beyond repair. Ask the service company whether it is worth repairing. Check out how much a

replacement appliance would cost from a warehouse seconds appliance shop. Often you get the same warranty period as you would if you paid full price.

- Can you pay household expenses like council rates in instalments? or can you pay the total up-front and get a discount? Read all your bills that come in and check out your options.

Family/children

- If babysitting is a big expense for you, start a babysitting club with friends.
- What jobs can your children do to earn their pocket money?
- Buy kids' clothes on sale at the end of the season and put them away for next year.
- From the moment our children were born we borrowed and passed on everything from baby clothes to baby bottles to school clothes – this saved thousands of dollars.

Medical/health and sport

- Instead of paying a big fitness club fee, make an exercise plan with friends – it's cheaper and you will probably stick to it because you have arranged to meet your friends or family members at an agreed time and place. If you join a club, can you get a free one-month trial? Can you pay in instalments? Can you pay less if there are services you won't use?
- What sports equipment do you really need? Can you buy sports shoes on sale? Can you sell the equipment you don't need any more?
- How much rebate can you get from your health fund?

Entertainment

- You can save on entertainment by going out midweek – movies, concerts and plays are all cheaper earlier in the week.
- Take videos and DVDs back on time so you don't pay a late fee. Use discount coupons whenever you can, and shop around – sometimes there can be price variations between stores.
- Join a movie club where you only pay $15 registration for the year and then get all the tickets at around $9 instead of $13 each time you go to the movies.

- Can you get discount vouchers for the entertainment you want to go to?
- Can you get together a group of 10 for the show or movie you want to see and receive a discount?
- If you decide to have pay TV, do you really need all the channels or is there a cheaper plan you could take?
- What about setting up a theatre group and subscribing for the year at a cheaper rate than buying individual tickets?

Food and eating out

- Take your lunch to work. Have a snack jar at work so you don't run out and spend $3 on a chocolate bar when you feel hungry in the afternoon.
- Restaurants often have midweek specials, or specials if you eat earlier in the evening. Does your favourite restaurant have discount coupons in the local paper or on shopping dockets?
- Make your coffee at work rather than buying takeaway coffee. Buy a cheap coffee pot and some good coffee – saving you time and money.
- Bulk buy basic household goods such as cleaning products, toilet paper and canned foods. Buy from a discount outlet and stock up so you don't get caught short and have to buy from the more expensive local shop.
- Regularly buying takeaway food can add up, as we saw in the Cash Diary. Cook on the weekend when you're relaxed and have more time, then stock up the fridge for the week. Make a big pot of soup and freeze it for when you get home from work and you're too tired to cook. If you don't or can't cook, get a friend to teach you or buy a simple cookbook and start experimenting. Home-cooked food is healthier as you know exactly what's going into it. Di told us when she and her partner stopped having takeaways they also had fewer cases of stomach virus. Saving $15 a night on takeaway food could work out to $75 dollars a week – $300 a month that could be going into investing for wealth creation.
- Start a fruit and vegie co-op. Five families pool their money, saving time and saving money on their fruit and vegie bill. Each week or fortnight one family goes to the market, does all the shopping, then at home splits it into five boxes, for each family to collect.

Clothes and personal items

- Only go shopping when the sales are on or only shop at the discount warehouse stores. Ask yourself whether you will really wear something and what else it goes with in your wardrobe, including shoes and handbags.
- Rather than buying expensive shampoos from the hairdressers, go to one of the many discount stores and stock up on the same products at the cheaper rate.
- Do you really need to get your hair cut every six weeks or can you wait a bit longer for your next visit?
- Don't buy clothes that say 'dry clean only' – if you do, you can buy your own dry cleaning fluid, 'Murex', which is great for spot cleaning your suits. If you have dry cleaning, take advantage of the cheaper rate if you have five items. Start a dry cleaning bag so you have enough items before you go to the dry cleaners.
- Get all your friends around for a clothing swap session – swap those wardrobe mistakes or clothes that don't fit you any longer.
- When you buy a new pair of shoes, get new nylon half soles put on them straight away – they'll last much longer.

Lifestyle and indulgences

- Cigarettes – cutting back on one packet a week can save you $15. See Chapter 5 on breaking bad habits if you need more convincing.
- The same with alcohol – do you need to buy a $10 cocktail at the bar or can you arrange to have drinks at home before you go out?
- Holidays – are you restricted when you can go, or can you arrange a holiday when it's not the peak period? Check out the internet for what packages there are. Look at house swapping options for holidays.
- Present box – instead of being in a mad panic to buy a gift, buy when you see things that would make great gifts on sale and keep them in a present box. Buy your wrapping and cards from the $2 stores. They have beautiful gift boxes, wrapping, cards and ribbons. Get your children to make personalised gift cards and wrapping. Use photos as cards.

Telecommunications

- Limit your mobile phone calls. Can the call wait until you get home and can ring at a cheaper rate? Change your habit to only use the phone to receive calls. Text messaging can be another expensive habit – it can be cheaper than a phone call to convey a simple essential message, but gets expensive when you get into a lengthy exchange of messages.
- Find out what networks your friends and family use – you may be able to get discounted or free calls to them at certain times.
- Change your mobile phone to pre-paid credit if you don't use your phone much.
- Review your mobile, phone and internet plans – can you get a cheaper deal elsewhere, or can you get a discount if you have all your plans with one provider?
- Each time your bill comes in, go through it and look at everything you are paying for. Mistakes can happen, or your company might advertise a cheaper rate for certain types of call at certain times, or new options that might suit you better.

Transport

- Do you really need to take a taxi? Can you get to the same place in a bus?
- Can you walk to work – get fit and save money as well!
- Do you really need to have the expense of owning a car! Just think of what you could do with the money saved from not owning a car? You can always hire a car if you need it on occasions. Can you get a 'novated lease' through your salary package from work?
- Check out the NRMA tips – for example, not using the air-conditioning and driving smoothly can save on petrol. Do you really need to go back to the car company for the service or can your local cheaper mechanic do the service?
- Keep tabs on petrol prices (from reputable stations) and fill up when it's cheap.

Financial

- Talk to your bank – how many credit cards and bank accounts do you have? Reduce them and save on fees and charges, not to mention paperwork.
- Speak to your bank regarding switching out of your home loan into a lower interest rate loan. Or look at fixing part or all of your interest rate (this makes for more certain repayments).
- How much are you paying for your insurance (car, home, life)? Check out the competition. Can you get it cheaper elsewhere? Make some investigations in your lunchtime and you could save hundreds of dollars.
- Many insurance companies will give a discount if you have all your insurance with one company.
- Are you paying a fee for your credit card – can you get a better deal elsewhere? Check out Chapter 5 on credit cards and what to look for.
- If you pay your credit card by the due date then check out the loyalty plans and what suits you. It can be a better deal to cash in your points for store vouchers rather than frequent flyer points that can be hard to redeem.

Here are some more tactics that we used to save and pay for our monthly contribution to our investment club, which has helped us to build our financial fitness:

- *'I never take more than $30 cash in my wallet when I go out. That way I'm never tempted.'*
- *'Each day I empty the small change from my wallet and put this in a box. At the end of every month I bank this amount, sometimes it's as much as $100.'*
- *'Every time I put something on my credit card, I write down the expense in my diary. This helps counter the feeling that it's not real money, and helps me budget for the bill at the end of the month.'*
- *'Whenever my credit card bill arrives, I put a note in my diary the day before it's due and make sure I pay it off in full. Interest on credit cards is very expensive and a complete waste of money.'*

- *'I made an agreement with my partner that if I wanted to buy something, like new clothes or something for the house, I would not do it on the spot but would wait until the end of the week before deciding if I really wanted it. I saved a huge amount by changing my behaviour and it helped me recognise my money triggers.'*

Identifying your money triggers

As with physical fitness, we are never going to be perfect in our financial fitness (remember, there are only eight supermodels in the world) but you can reduce these sidetracks by knowing your money triggers. Go back to your Cash Diary or Money Picture and ask yourself – when have you spent money on things you really didn't need? Can you identify the trigger? If you're having a bad day at work, do you hit the shops at lunchtime to compensate or put on a bet at the TAB? Imagine how it would feel to walk past the rubbish bin and throw a $50 note in there. Isn't this what you are doing by buying something you are never going to wear or putting on a bet which in all probability won't win?

Our money triggers are made all the more easy to indulge when we don't even need to have money in our wallet. When you pay cash you see the money going out of your wallet, but not so with a credit card because your card is given back to you after your purchase. Would you make the same purchase if you were paying cash out of your wallet? Would this make you stop? When you buy something on credit imagine the money coming out of your wallet – visualise the $50 note.

Awareness of your particular money triggers is the first step; the next is to try out some distractions. Go for a walk (*not* past the shops), ring a friend, read the newspaper, make an agreement with your partner not to buy spontaneously, knowing that you can go back if you really need it, update your Money Picture and remind yourself of the path you are on. It won't work every time but for the times it does, it's worth it.

Now you have identified your triggers there are some other money strategies you can use to stay on track.

Staying on track

How many expenses have you cut back on during the month after going through the Money Picture? Let's say after cutting back, you can save $100 per month. How are you going to maintain this and where are you going to put it?

If you know that you may easily fall back to your old habits then have the money automatically taken out of your salary. Your employer can arrange this or you can arrange for your bank to put a direct transfer every month into a deposit account that you can't access for a period of time, such as a term deposit account.

A simple strategy is to direct your pay into two separate bank accounts.

1. The 'can't touch' bank account

An amount of your pay is put directly into this bank account and cannot be touched except for the purposes that you've set. Maybe it's a term deposit account, or perhaps you get your mortgage or loan repayments paid directly from this account.

It could be a regular bank account but the amount you have taken out of your pay is enough to cover your fixed expenses for the year. This might be rent, electricity, school fees, telephone, car expenses, insurance, etc – the items your Money Picture shows you have to pay. Or perhaps you could put this amount directly into a managed investment fund so you can grow your wealth.

2. The 'active' bank account for weekly expenses

Only the remainder of your pay goes into this account to cover everything else you spend money on; go back to your Money Picture and have a look at what these are. Expenses may include groceries, cigarettes, alcohol, babysitting, going out, new clothes, entertainment.

Here is the catch – if you run out you cannot touch the other account. You must wait until the following pay period.

When your Money Diet goes off the rails

We will all have times when we go off the rails! What's important is how you cope with your financial setback, be it of your own making, such as an unplanned spending spree, or maybe something you couldn't see coming, such as expensive car repairs or a large electricity or phone bill. It's painful to have to dig into our savings, or worse still, to have to borrow money to pay for these surprise expenses. What can we do about them?

Firstly, build some 'fat' or risk margin into your Money Diet. Overestimate how much you expect things will cost. It's a bit like overestimating the number of calories you've eaten in the day or going for a run instead of a walk. This applies particularly to categories such as car repairs, where it's difficult to predict how much you'll have to spend in any year. Set aside an amount every month for your money fat to cover these unexpected expenses.

Another way of coping is to pay off the bill over a period of time, to avoid more expensive means of finding the money such as a cash advance on your credit card. Council rates are an example of a bill you can pay in instalments.

If the setback is an unplanned spending spree, think carefully about what might have triggered it. Can you work out a strategy to avoid it happening again? For example, you could cut up your credit card, or impose a cooling-off period on yourself before making any major spending decisions. Have another look at your money triggers.

If it seems as though you have nothing but one setback after another, and never an opportunity to make up your savings, have a closer look at these expenses from your Money Picture. Are they all really unexpected? On the other hand, could at least some of the expenses have been anticipated? For example, you might have to get new tyres for your car for it to pass registration. This is not really an unexpected expense, in that you know your car will need new tyres from time to time. It's just something you'd prefer not to think about until you're forced to, and then you have to pay for the tyres at short notice and usually top price.

Now you have your Money Cycle as a tool you can look at the future and make decisions. Once you start on your Money Diet and have more and more money left at the end of each cycle, congratulations – you're moving into Green. Now you can use that extra money to build your wealth – don't leave it just sitting in the bank, it needs to be out there working for your financial fitness!

CHAPTER 5

Breaking bad habits

Now we are going to look at some specific issues that might be stopping you from achieving your goals. You've done your financial Health Check, and you know if you are Red, Amber or Green. You've written down your goals, and the next step is to plan how you are going to achieve them. Do you have any bad habits that are costing you more than you think?

Regardless of whether you are Red, Amber or Green, look at the everyday habits that might be costing you dearly. In some cases, that cost could make the difference between Red and Amber, or even Amber and Green. The way you use your credit cards, or the unnecessary or even harmful things you spend your money on, could be costing you thousands of dollars each year. Some of these bad habits may even be doing irreparable damage to your greatest asset – your own health.

Everyday indulgences such as buying scratchies, smoking, drinking or splurging on new clothes may seem small items, but as you know from doing the Health Check and Money Picture, these expenses can quickly add up. This is like money just draining (or disappearing) out of your wallet.

We all like to have a good time and we do not believe that cutting out all the things you enjoy just to save money is worthwhile in the longer term. It's up to you to determine how bad your bad habits really are, so you can make an informed choice knowing the full costs.

Overspending on credit cards

If you're worried that your spending is out of control, that you're over your head in debt, chances are that a credit card is one of the major causes. Credit cards are fast becoming the most common way of buying things and paying bills. They are incredibly convenient and seductive. Credit cards are very easy to get – almost anyone can get one, regardless of your ability to repay. Credit card purchases can give us a false sense of security – perhaps because we don't see and feel the money being taken from our wallets.

Losing control of your spending through overuse of credit cards is a major and common financial trap. It's fairly easy to pick up a home loan with an interest rate of 6%–7%, but when you apply for a credit card you'll most likely find that the interest rate is around a massive 17.5%. If you are not paying off your credit card each month, then you are in effect taking out a very high-interest loan.

Credit cards are not inherently evil and some people have worked out ways to use them effectively. For instance, you may find it very convenient to put all your expenses on a credit card, so that you get reward points and have one record of your expenses that is easy to check.

The key is to be able to pay off the full balance on time and not to get caught in the interest trap. If you have trouble paying off your credit card debt each month and you are accumulating an ongoing and growing interest bill it can cost you hundreds or even thousands of dollars each year. For example, a credit card debt of $5000 will cost approximately $72 in interest every month and that amount increases for every month it's not paid. If you are in this situation don't panic – in this chapter we have some practical ideas to help you get out of this costly cycle and back on track.

Five years ago three-quarters of Australians paid off their credit card debt each month. Now only a quarter of Australians pay off their credit card every month and, according to *BRW* (March 2002), the average debt per adult is now $2073, an increase of 12%

over the past 12 months. This means that the majority of people are not paying off their high-interest 'loan' and are carrying it as an increasing bad debt. If this sounds like you then you need to take action to make sure that you reduce your spending and get into a position to be able to pay off your credit card debt.

Reducing credit card pain

The first task is to clear your debt so that you are not carrying forward interest. The key to doing this is to manage your cashflow, i.e. to have more going in every month to pay off the card than is being added on as extra purchases.

Bronwyn, who is 28, earns a good salary, but she realised that most of it seemed to get spent on lifestyle activities that she charged to her credit card. She didn't have any major assets to show for all her hard work.

I have been working for about seven years and have always had good jobs. I have a university degree and earn reasonably good money. I realised about six months ago that I didn't seem to be able to save anything at all. I became a bit depressed because I spoke to some of my friends and they seemed to have all sorts of investments organised. I have not been able to put any money aside. I started to really analyse where my money was going – it is not like I earn a lot more or less than my friends. I realised that I was using my credit card to fund my lifestyle – spending my money on work clothes, shoes, lunches, social activities, holidays – I guess disposable things that have no ongoing value. I hadn't really analysed it – I just paid the bills each month. I started to really budget seriously. I decided not to use my credit card for anything except bills like telephone and electricity – not for clothes, shoes and so on. I use cash and I've started to buy cheaper shirts and stopped buying designer labels of anything. I always thought that I needed them for work but no-one has even noticed.

Because I am now paying with cash, it is much more difficult to spend a lot. I've been far more careful about buying things like shoes and only buy at the end of the season – which means that I get great shoes for half the price! I've also really changed my social activities and only go to expensive bars and restaurants once a month – and then I am more careful about what I order. I was shocked at the difference this made.

This discipline of changing my habits and only using cash seems to have worked so far and amazingly without too much pain – in fact I don't even notice it now. It's actually fun and a challenge to try and find a good bargain. I have managed to save nearly $5000 and am now looking at various investment options. I feel like I have really achieved something – and it wasn't that hard!

If you receive an offer in the mail for a new credit card, or an increased limit, think carefully if you can afford it. Watch out if your capacity to take on credit card debt is constantly expanding – it will be much harder for you to limit your credit card use. These offers are not a vote of confidence in you by your bank. They are an attempt to extract more money from you in the form of annual fees and high interest. It is a marketing exercise and its sole purpose is to make more money for the bank.

Once you've got your balance down to zero, or an amount you know you can pay off completely every month, think about whether you want to go back to using your credit card again. Can you trust yourself not to let your spending get out of hand? Do you have the discipline to pay off the balance every month? Do you know how much you can afford to put on your card every month?

Analyse the way you have been using your credit card or cards; go through your statements from the last six months, and separate out the different items according to the categories from your Financial Health Check (e.g. telephone, electricity, entertainment, etc). You should now know whether you are overspending on your credit card. If you are overspending, then you need to look at your spending habits and work out what is essential and what is discretionary spending. Maybe Bronwyn's strategy will work for you, to only use your credit card for essential bills such as telephone and electricity, and to use cash for discretionary spending such as clothes and entertainment.

Rationalising your credit cards is important. Get rid of them all if you have to – start with the ones that cost you most in fees and interest. You may decide you need to cut them out altogether.

If it's too late and you are already saddled with a credit card debt you can't clear in a month, there are things you can do right now to lessen the pain. Some banks will transfer your credit card debt onto an alternative card where you are eligible for lower interest rate repayments. This will give you some time and space to plan and pay off the debt while taking advantage of a lower interest rate. The lower rate will only apply for a limited period of time, so use that as a deadline for getting the balance down to zero, if you can.

You could also look to shifting to an overdraft on a savings account or a low interest personal loan. The objective is to consolidate your debt into an arrangement that has a lower interest rate, so that the repayments you make can pay off the principal faster.

Until you have got your credit card balance down to an amount that can be paid off completely in a month, don't add on any more purchases to the card. Don't take your credit card with you when you go out; that way you won't be tempted. If you can't afford to pay cash now, how can you afford to pay the purchase price plus maybe 17% interest?

The most important thing is to work out how you can pay off your credit card debt, and if this seems difficult, contact the financial institution that issued the card to get help as soon as possible.

Barrier buster

If the temptation is too much, cut up your credit cards. You can always apply for a new one once your finances are back on track.

Choosing the right credit card

Credit cards are actually extremely useful if they are managed effectively. They avoid bank fees, are convenient and secure, and offer a charge-back service in case of fraud.

There are more than 200 different types of credit card available – all with different payment options, charges, interest rates, and loyalty and incentive programs. Working out which one is best for you and your needs can be complicated. When choosing a credit card you need to work out why you need it and whether you really need all the facilities offered. There are a growing number of 'no frills' credit cards being offered by smaller banks and other institutions. These are now available with interest rates far lower than the cards that have loyalty and other programs attached. The more that is offered with each card, the more you will pay, either by way of annual fee or by inflated interest charges. For example, a credit card with no loyalty points could offer an interest rate around 5% lower than other cards or cost much less in fees each year.

If you are paying off your credit card each month then the interest rate won't matter, but the reward scheme and associated perks, as well as the annual fee, will be very relevant.

The Australian Consumers Association (ACA) has a service and a website (www.choice.com.au) that analyses the different options on various different credit cards.

Barrier buster

Look at what you are really getting from your card's loyalty program – it is rarely worth spending money just to gain points. For example, you could spend as much as $17,000 just to earn a flight from Sydney to Melbourne, when if you plan your timing right, you can buy a fare for as little as $77 one way. Think carefully whether you are spending just to build up frequent flyer points.

THE ADVANTAGES OF HAVING A CREDIT CARD
- Flexibility and convenience
- Enables shopping and bill paying by phone
- Gives worldwide coverage
- Up to 55 days interest-free period with some cards
- Extra protection if you have a dispute

- Some offer loyalty programs
- Some also give extra warranty and insurance
- No need to carry large amounts of cash
- Liability can be limited if your card is used fraudulently
- Enables you to avoid transaction fees levied with debit and cheque accounts

THE DISADVANTAGES OF HAVING A CREDIT CARD

- High interest rates
- Expensive for long-term borrowing compared to personal loans
- Cards with loyalty programs usually have higher interest rates and fees
- If you don't pay back your total balance each month, the interest charged can actually end up doubling the cost of your original purchase
- If you're not good at budgeting and managing your finances, the overuse of credit cards can leave you with a debt that's very difficult to pay back

Jan is 32 and was a credit card fan until she looked at the maths.

I thought that it was such a wonderful way of tracking my expenditure and gave me freedom. It wasn't until my boyfriend went through my statements for a year and shocked me with the full calculation of interest that I was paying that I really took any notice. I was just throwing away around two thousand dollars just on interest repayments because I wasn't paying off the full amount on my credit card by the due date each month. As soon as I found this out I started to really monitor what I put on my credit card and tried to use cash. I also made sure that I organised telephone and internet banking so I pay off the full amount each month. I put myself on really strict controls for spending. Finding that out and working out what I was spending my money on really changed the way I used my credit card and my priorities. I now use a cash system and only use credit card for paying bills. I found that it is not that hard and you really do notice that money going out of the wallet!

ASSESSING YOUR OWN CREDIT CARD

- What is the number of days between receiving the bill and your deadline for payment – i.e. the interest-free period – does it fit with when you are paid?
- How easy is it to pay your credit card – can you get the amount taken out of your account each month? This will eliminate the risk of not paying on time.
- What is the interest rate charged?
- What are the annual fees and other charges? Once you have looked at the costs work out what you really need. Maybe the fees don't make the programs such as insurance or loyalty programs cost-effective.

Alternatives to credit cards

These days, paying cash doesn't necessarily mean you have to walk around with bundles of notes in your wallet. You can still enjoy the convenience of paying electronically, without the interest charges. Most shops will accept EFTPOS payments, and bills can be paid from savings or cheque accounts on the phone or internet using BPay.

Debit cards are another alternative to credit cards. These cards are issued by Visa and MasterCard, the major credit card companies. You can use them at shops and supermarkets, and to pay bills by phone or internet. They are just like credit cards, except that you are not putting anything on credit; the cards are linked to a savings account and will only work if there is enough money in the account to cover the purchase. Every month you will get a monthly statement, listing all your purchases, but you won't have to pay off the statement; the money will already have been taken out of your account to pay for your purchases, and the balance showing on the statement should always be a credit balance.

You can also use debit cards to get cash at ATMs overseas, provided there is enough money in the linked account. Unlike credit cards, there are no loyalty programs, annual fees or interest charges.

Debit cards have all the convenience of credit cards, without the potential for overspending and massive interest charges. They are perfect for anyone who is trying to give up a bad credit card habit but loves the convenience of paying with plastic.

Store credit and 'interest-free' items

Most department stores will have their own in-house form of credit card, with an even higher rate of interest than those issued by banks. Obviously, everything we have said here about credit cards applies equally to store cards.

Another way that stores can lure you into debt is by offering interest-free terms on major purchases, usually for one to two years. These offers are linked to finance companies, and once the interest-free period expires, the interest rate is huge, usually more than 20% per annum.

Frances found that it's possible to avoid paying interest, but you have to be very careful.

I needed to upgrade my computer, and opted for a 12 month interest-free arrangement. You paid one third of the cost up-front, another third in monthly instalments over the 12 months, and the final third in another lump sum when the 12 months expired. Any amounts outstanding at the end of the period incurred interest at an extremely high rate, which I had no intention of paying; I planned to have the whole amount paid by then.

As the 12 month anniversary approached, I expected that the finance company would send me some sort of final statement. This didn't happen, so I rang them up to check the date and ask what I had to do to make the final payment. It was quite hard to get through on the phone (in the end I selected the phone menu item for increasing my credit limit – they answered that one!) and although they didn't exactly discourage me from paying the whole amount off, they didn't go out of their way to make it easy either. I never received anything from them to remind me that the amount was due or stating when interest would start to run.

This type of payment option worked out well for me, but only because I was extremely careful not to let the final payment date slip by. The system was set up to make it very easy not to notice that the interest-free period had passed.

Tips for using your credit card

1. Only have one credit card and track your statements carefully.
2. Shop around – there is a huge variety in what is offered. For example, check interest-free days to pay off the bill, interest rates, card application fees, yearly fees and other charges.
3. If you can't pay off the full amount each month, at least pay off an amount that well exceeds the minimum payment, thereby reducing the outstanding balance.
4. Don't increase your credit limit unless you can *really* afford it.
5. Avoid any kind of cash advance – you'll be paying interest from the date of the advance.
6. If you are deep in credit card debt, negotiate manageable repayment rates with the credit card company or look at how you can work with a bank which offers you a lower interest rate for a few months so that you can pay off your debt.
7. Avoid using credit cards at all until your debt is paid off.
8. If you cannot repay your debt contact your financial institution immediately.
9. Keep your credit card in an organiser, so every time you use it, you can straightaway write down the cost. This makes the purchase seem more like spending real money, and the bill at the end of the month won't come as a nasty surprise.
10. If you have an interest-free period, keep track of the statement date and try to make most of your purchases at the beginning of the cycle, to maximise the number of interest free days.
11. Especially if you plan to make a major purchase, defer it until the first day of a new interest cycle.
12. Check all statements carefully – compare them to the list in your organiser. Contact the bank straightaway if you spot an unauthorised transaction.

Credit cards in themselves are not the problem. The problem is overspending, and credit cards are the means by which people can overspend, way beyond their capacity to repay, for an extended period of time, before reality catches up. Three-quarters of credit card users (those who pay interest) are subsidising the other quarter (who don't pay interest). It's obvious which category to aim for.

Adding up the real costs of addictions

Just as overspending on your credit card can be a form of addiction, there are other types of addictions and bad habits that can be ruinous to your finances.

Addictions are extremely costly emotionally, physically and financially, not just to the person concerned but to their family, friends, and the community in general. Addictions to cigarettes, alcohol, illicit drugs and gambling affect a large number of Australians and their families. Now that you have taken steps to analyse and take control of your finances you may need to look at your bad habits or addictions.

Any of us who drink or smoke tend to think that it is pleasurable, worthwhile and doesn't cost much. But you might be surprised if you sit down and work out how much you and your family spend on 'bad habits' or addictions each year. It is relatively simple to work out the direct costs: for example, if you smoke one packet of cigarettes each day then over a year it will directly cost you around $4000.

It is also worth considering what we might call the 'indirect' costs of addictions. The indirect costs include illness and short or long-term damage to your health which may mean you are not able to work for a period of time. The statistics show that there is an increase in the likelihood of a major health problem or even death if you smoke or drink a great deal. Don't forget that the likelihood of increased health costs will also spill over into higher premiums for life and income protection insurance. These factors are the ones that most people choose to ignore – but they obviously have a major impact not only on your health but also on your earning capacity.

Tobacco

The direct cost of smoking is huge – and just think, most of it goes to the government; a form of voluntary taxation! The $4000 you'll pay each year to smoke a packet a day comes out of your after-tax income, so depending on your tax rate this could mean that you need to earn up to $8000 extra each year to pay for your addiction. By giving up smoking you may be able to change your financial position quite dramatically.

This is just the start; you also have to add on the additional costs of sickness and the impact on your health and the health of others around you.

Everyone knows that smoking can kill you; in fact the risk of death from tobacco is more than *eight times* greater than the lifelong risk of death from traffic accidents, suicide, homicide, AIDS and illicit drug abuse *combined*.

It's hard to give up smoking because it's so addictive (if it is any consolation, rock star David Bowie said in a radio interview that it was harder for him to give up smoking tobacco than taking heroin), but the situation becomes more urgent once you realise that your health is starting to fail.

Carol is now 52. She smoked for many years and it wasn't until she got extremely ill that she really took her addiction seriously. This was a strong incentive to give up and it worked.

I used to smoke. I worked out that it only cost me about $1500 each year to smoke and I enjoyed it very much. So the cost seemed worth the pleasure. What I didn't realise until I got very ill is all the harmful side effects that we ignore.

Cancer is an obvious thing thrown at smokers and something I believed would never happen to me – it hasn't yet. What did happen was that my immune system seemed to be permanently damaged. I caught every bug going around and had a lot of time off work. This led to a loss of income because I actually used up all my sick leave and my holidays. The combination of health costs seemed suddenly to be huge and my quality of life was poor. I started working out what I could afford to 'risk' and then realised that I couldn't risk my health. When I was sick I not only felt bad but I was very restricted in what I could do. I gave up smoking. I went on a program run by a local hospital and there was a great support network. It was extremely hard work – one of the hardest things I have ever done. I am proud to say that I achieved my goal and have given up. By doing this I saved a lot of money. I have really focused now on my health and feel that I've done this successfully!

Alcohol

Like smoking, alcohol also has direct and indirect costs. This includes the direct costs of buying drinks and also the indirect costs such as damage to your health. Have you ever taken a day off work because of a bad hangover? It's estimated that five in every 100 workers are alcohol-dependent, with another 20 drinking heavily enough to put them at risk. These statistics are scary, and if you recognise yourself or someone in your family you need to take action.

Illicit and prescription drugs

Here we are talking about cannabis, cocaine, amphetamines, heroin, hallucinogens, ecstasy and a lot of other 'pharmaceuticals' such as morphine, codeine, pethidine and methadone. Some of these drugs are extremely addictive – not to mention costly. There are also some prescription drugs that, when abused, can be just as hard to give up; for instance, some types of tranquillisers and sleeping tablets. Although they can be a useful short-term treatment for some conditions, it is very easy to become inadvertently addicted.

Gambling

Gambling is another very costly activity and, for many, an addiction. Gambling includes betting on the pokies, horses, lotteries, scratchies and casino gaming. Poker machines, which are now in many pubs as well as clubs, make up around 76% of the total amount spent by problem gamblers. It is extremely easy to gamble – the quick pull of the pokie here and the lottery ticket there and the promise of getting rich quick. There is a lot of evidence that suggests that gambling will dramatically affect your productivity at work and your home life. Gambling is given as a major reason for divorce, depression and even suicide.

Gambling costs the average problem gambler between $6000 and $19,000 per year. This is a great deal of money and will have an obvious impact on your financial position.

Where to go for help

We aren't telling you anything you haven't read or seen on television. Addictions are a serious medical, social and financial problem. If you recognise yourself (or perhaps a friend or someone in your family) in this chapter you need to get some specialist help. Looking just at the financial impact of addictions, it's clear that you won't be able to get your finances under control until you or your partner or family member can get the addictive behaviour in control.

Credit cards

There are numerous organisations specifically set up to help people work through problems with credit cards, including:

- www.choice.com.au is an online information service which provides a comprehensive list of rates and charges for banking products including credit cards.
- Credit Helpline (1800 808 488) is a free financial counselling service. They provide experienced counsellors who talk to people over the phone and refer them to a service close to where they live. Free face-to-face counselling is also available. Visit Wesley Mission's Credit Line website for more information on their financial counselling services – www.wesleymission. org.au/centres/creditline
- The Financial Counsellors' Association of NSW website (www.acwa.asn.au/fcan) helps you find a financial counsellor near you, including interstate numbers.
- You can locate financial counsellors in country NSW locations by visiting www.ruralcounselling.org.au
- Lifeline is an international organisation offering a free telephone counselling service – contact them on 13 11 14.

- Debtors Anonymous is a group much like Alcoholics Anonymous. They consider compulsive spending as serious an addiction as drugs or alcohol and consider denial to be the biggest part of the addiction. Like drug taking, spending produces an instant reward, and if stopped, the person affected will suffer withdrawal symptoms. Check in your local phone book to see if there is a meeting near you.

Alcohol

There are many organisations you can go to for help, including Alcoholics Anonymous, who run group meetings in most towns and cities. Visit www.aa.org.au or telephone (02) 9599 8866 – this is the National Office, which will be able to put you in contact with help in your area. Lifeline can also help you find services in your local area (13 11 14), or look in the community pages of your phone book.

Tobacco

There are numerous support groups to help people give up smoking. Visit the Quit website at www.quitnow.info.au or call the national Quitline on 13 18 48. Quit offers a huge range of support and practical help including quit packs, advisers or counsellors, information for students as well as information on tobacco.

Gambling

For help with gambling, try Gamblers Anonymous at www.gamblersanonymous.org.au or call their national telephone number on (02) 9550 0430.

There's also the G-Line, a free telephone counselling service for problem gamblers and their families. Phone 1800 633 635 (NSW); 1800 222 050 (Qld); 1800 000 973 (Tas); 1800 156 789 (Vic); 1800 060 757 (SA); 1800 622 112 (WA).

CHAPTER 6

The basics of investing

A few years back if someone had called us investors we would have laughed and said, 'Not us!' We are investors today because we took the time to learn. We found out that it wasn't as hard as we thought and we didn't need as much money as we'd imagined. Our investment club started with us contributing just $50 per month.

Today, we are investors with financial goals to achieve. From our experiences we have learnt not just about shares but also about other ways of investing. Investing is the way to build your financial fitness, so let's start with some training on the basics of investing and then look at where you might want to invest and how to do it.

First, try this word association game. Sit down and close your eyes and think of the words *investor* and *investments* – let pictures and words come into your head. Then write them all down.

What did your word association game show?

- Did you have an image of someone other than yourself? Perhaps it was an image of a share broker in a fine suit? Or a hectic stock exchange?
- Did you say things like 'I don't understand' or 'How do I start?'
- Did you picture the investments you have or would like to have?

Now try this . . .

Picture yourself in one year's time, sitting in the same place. You are making monthly additional contributions towards your superannuation fund. Or you might be putting $50 each month into a Christmas saver account or managed share fund. Perhaps you have bought an investment property or started an investment club, as we did.

You are *now an investor* and you have *investments* from which you can earn an income, and make a profit as the value of your investments grows through capital gain (the difference between the buying price and the selling price). As an investor, you are making your money work for you.

This chapter gives you the basics of investing. It's not intended to give you investment advice but to answer questions like: What is investing? What is risk? How long do I have to invest for? How will I make money from investments? Can I lose my money? What do all those technical words mean?

Once you have the basic building blocks of investment in place, you can move on to where to invest and really start to build your wealth.

What is investing?

Investing means making a decision about putting your money into cash, property or shares so that you can make an income now and/or a profit later. Sounds easy? Let's take a closer look.

The three main investment classes are:

1. **Cash or fixed interest** – where you put money into a cash account such as a savings account or term deposit, and keep it there to earn interest.
2. **Property** – where you buy a property, be it a house, unit, garage, office or shop, and you earn rental income from the property or make a profit through selling it for a higher price than you paid for it.
3. **Shares** – where you have part ownership in an Australian or overseas company that is listed on the stock exchange.

There are other investment areas outside of cash, property and shares, such as art works and racehorses. The basics of investing apply equally to all types.

What is risk?

Which do you think has a higher risk: buying shares or putting your money in the bank? Would you expect to be paid more if you take a greater risk? Everyone's intention is to make money from investing, but many don't. Why? Usually because they don't understand risk and return and want to make some quick easy money.

Risk means that there is a chance that you will not get what you expected to get (the return). Remember, no investment is completely 'risk free'. Risk and return go hand in hand and are important in making real life decisions on where to invest your money. Low return usually means lower risk; high return means higher risk.

How much you are prepared to risk will depend on your reason for investing. If you want to invest in the short term with ready access to your money, you might choose something low risk and low return such as a savings account or term deposit; if you're looking to save a deposit for a house in five years, you might choose something with slightly higher risk and good returns but not too much volatility; if you're looking to invest for the long term, you can balance out the risks over time, so higher-risk investment products with the possibility of high returns might be best for you.

Look at the graph on the next page, which shows risk level for the three main classes of investments. Not surprisingly, the fixed security of cash has lowest risk and lowest return, followed by bonds, whereas property sits between cash and shares, and shares have the highest return at the highest risk.

What is return?

There are two ways to make money out of investments: income and capital gain. Income could take the form of interest earned on cash

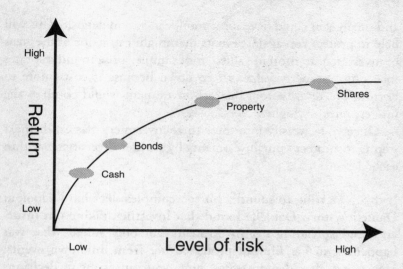

in an account, rent from a property, or dividends paid on shares. Some types of investment will increase in value and produce a capital gain as well. This means that someone will pay more for the investment today than the price you paid previously. The difference between the purchase and selling price is called the capital gain (or capital loss if the amount is negative). You don't necessarily have to choose between earning income and making a capital gain; with property and shares, you will hopefully do both.

What is diversification?

You can reduce your risk and maximise your returns by splitting your money into a number of different investments; this is called *diversification*. Remember the saying, 'Don't put all your eggs in one basket'? Why wouldn't you? Because if the basket is dropped, you potentially break the lot. So, what does that mean for you in investing? If you put all your money into one investment, and that investment goes bad, you lose your money.

In investing, you diversify or spread your risk by putting your money into the different baskets of cash, property and shares. You might own your own house, which is an investment in property. Maybe you have superannuation in a fund that invests in shares;

and finally you could have some money in a term deposit. This will help to protect you against events that might cause one of the areas of investment to drop in value – for example, a rise in interest rates may cause property values to go down because it costs more to borrow, but returns from the cash investment would go up as the interest rates are higher.

Once you diversify into these three investment classes, the next step is to protect your investments by further diversifying within each class.

If this is starting to sound a bit too complex, let's have a look at Danielle's story. Danielle found that investing, taking out insurance and spreading her investments not only suited what was happening in her life but protected her from unknown events. Her story also demonstrates how your investment decisions change with your circumstances.

After I divorced my second husband, I was left with two children and a good job, but no superannuation or savings. I decided to see a financial planner. I organised this through my company, as I knew they were setting up a super scheme for their employees. The planner helped me set up my own super scheme; we also set up trauma insurance (which was the best thing I ever did) and income protection insurance.

I continued working and kept up with my finances. I bought a house, acquired my first share and had a modest portfolio. Having a home for myself and my boys was the most important priority for me, as well as building my investments.

I'm in my forties now and was recently diagnosed with breast cancer. I am so glad I kept up the payments with my trauma insurance. I received a lump sum payout and put the money into various interest-bearing bank deposits and bonds. I didn't want to risk the volatility of the share market, I needed to have the assurance I could access the money for more treatments.

Eighteen months ago, I started to invest in a managed fund. I really like managed funds – if you pick the right ones you get enough exposure to the various markets and can leave the worry to the experts. That's not to say you don't check on the performances of your funds – you still need to be able to change your mix and invest in better performing funds.

I also make extra contributions towards my company super fund. This is great as it's paid before I get my salary so I don't even miss the money.

Now my main financial goal is to minimise my tax. I'm looking to negative gear and have decided that an investment property is a good way to do this. The location will be the main consideration; I want to ensure good, ongoing rentals.

Going through my second divorce was the turning point for me, as I discovered I had to be responsible for my own finances. I tell others to educate themselves, read books, read magazines and talk to the experts. Just start.

Getting started

Now you are comfortable with the basics of investing, the next step is to ask some questions, gather all the answers and information you need, and then make decisions for your financial fitness.

First, ask yourself:

- What are my goals?
- How much money do I have to invest?
- What is my attitude to risk?
- How much time do I have to manage my investments?

You may not have felt the need to ask yourself these questions before, but with help from the chapters on goals, your financial Health Check and what's holding you back and why, now is your opportunity to answer them, so you can find out which investing options will work best for your particular circumstances.

The rest of this chapter will help you understand the characteristics of the three investment classes – cash, property and shares. These include the risk and return, complexity, tax issues and options within that class.

1. Cash or fixed interest

This type of investment will suit you if you are looking for certainty as it is low risk – but the other side of the equation is that you earn a lower return from the interest paid. The aim of investing is to make an income stream and a capital gain. This class gives you no capital gain but it does give you certainty in getting back the amount you invested plus an income stream of interest. Fixed term investments are good where you want the discipline of not being able to access your money for a period of time. Cash or fixed interest investments will also suit you if you need to be certain of getting the full amount you have invested back after a set period of time. In the case study earlier, Danielle put her money in bank deposits and bonds because she needed the certainty of getting all her money back when she had to pay for her cancer treatments, but she still managed to get a better interest rate than putting it in an everyday savings account.

Cash or fixed interest is one option for saving to meet short-term goals or to accumulate the larger amount you might need for future investments, such as an initial purchase of shares.

What is it?

Cash or fixed interest means putting money in a cash account (and keeping it there). It could be a savings plan or a fixed interest investment, which means that you invest for a set period of time to earn a fixed interest rate. For instance, with a one-year term deposit you agree to deposit money with the bank for one year without touching it, in return for a higher rate of interest than the bank would pay for your everyday transaction account.

Bonds are another type of fixed interest investment. When you buy a bond, which is issued by the government, it means you are lending money to the government, and they will repay the original money at the maturity date and also pay interest at certain times during the life (term) of the bond – that's why they come under the fixed interest investments class.

You can also get a fixed interest investment from corporations who issue *debentures*. Debentures are not as common as they used to be because companies tend to raise money from shares rather than by issuing debentures. The debenture offers a fixed interest rate usually secured by a specific asset of the company to secure the repayment of the amount you invested at an agreed date. Debentures are less risky than shares but have a lower rate of return.

How much do I need?

The advantage of cash and fixed interest investments is that you only need a small amount to start investing, although some term deposits have a minimum amount, as do bonds and debentures.

What is the risk?

Overall, as we saw in the risk chart in the basics of investing, this class has low risk. The risk varies between banks, building societies, credit unions, government bonds and secured debentures. The lowest risk is with Australian banks because the banking industry has special controls (called prudential regulation). Other financial institutions such as building societies and credit unions are not subject to the same level of controls but they pay a higher rate of interest. Government bonds are similarly low risk because the government undertakes to repay them, but the amount you need to invest is usually higher than for a bank term deposit. Debentures have a higher level of risk depending upon the company and the interest repayment.

When can I get my money back?

If it's a cash bank account then you can access your money any time. If it's fixed interest then it depends upon the type: government bonds and debentures are typically for longer periods and with less flexible time periods to select from than the fixed term products available at the bank.

What return will I get?

Your return will be in the form of an interest payment. In addition, you will have a high level of guarantee of getting back the original amount you invested. Interest will often be higher the longer you can fix the investment period for and the more money you can initially lock in.

There's also the effect of *compound interest*, which means you earn interest on the interest. For example, if you have $1000 in the bank earning 1% interest every month (i.e. 12% per annum), at the end of the first month you would have $1000 principal plus $10 interest, so the next month your interest would be worked out on principal of $1010. Every month both the principal and interest will increase. (This assumes interest is paid monthly. Our assumed interest rate of 1% per month is higher than what you would earn in real life, but easy to calculate by way of example.)

How complex is it?

Cash and fixed interest are the least complex of the three classes. Bank deposit and fixed term deposits are the least complex within this class; government bonds and debentures are more complex because you buy these investments through the 'money market' via a dealer or on the 'stock exchange' through a broker.

You can also put your money into a managed fund that invests in cash and fixed interest securities, where you pay a fee for professional managers to pool and manage the money for you – see information on managed funds further on in this chapter.

How is it taxed?

Interest income is taxable for income tax purposes at your personal tax rate.

What are my options?

For this class, where you invest will depend on how much money you have, when you want it back and how much money you can make by way of interest. There are different investments you can make in fixed interest products at the bank, and if you have a larger amount, you might look for a higher rate through a bond or debenture. Where do you have your money sitting? Even moving your cash out of a low interest rate savings account into a higher fixed interest account is worthwhile. To find the right product for you, check with various banks, building societies and credit unions. This is easiest to do on the internet, or you can check the comparative tables in newspapers and financial magazines. Compare interest rates, fees, conditions, ease of access to your money, and how often interest is calculated and paid (the more often the better).

2. Property

Australians have a high level of home ownership, and we often feel emotionally attached to our home. This can mean we don't see our homes strictly as an investment, but it's usually our biggest asset. This investment class is good if you are in a position to pay off a mortgage and want to hold the asset for a reasonable period of time and then earn a capital gain when you sell it.

What is it?

You are investing in property if you buy or own a property, be it a house, unit, garage, office or shop. You have a 'land title' or some legally recognised title to ownership.

How much do I need?

You will need at least some of your own money for a deposit, then most often you would borrow money to fund the rest of the purchase price. You'll also have to budget for stamp duty, legal and borrowing costs. If you are borrowing money, you need an income source to be able to meet the repayments on the mortgage, and the property must be worth at least 5%–20% more than the amount you have borrowed, so there is a cushion for the lender if you can't repay the money and the property has to be sold quickly. If you already own another property (for example, your house or flat), you can use that property as security as well, and borrow a higher proportion of the amount you need to buy the second property.

If you are not in a position to buy a property an alternative is to buy into a property trust, which is like a managed fund, where the investors' money is pooled, but instead of buying shares, the fund manager buys property. This can be an affordable way to invest in commercial property. Over time, as the value of the property goes up, the rent you receive should also increase; however, it's also possible in times of recession that rents can drop. See the section on managed funds later in this chapter.

What is the risk?

Historically, property prices are not as volatile as shares, so the level of risk sits between cash and shares. This means that although prices will go up and down, the 'up and down trends' are not as exaggerated and will stretch out over longer periods of time. When you buy investment property, you expect to earn an income in the form of rent, and also to make a capital gain as the value of the property increases. The risk may be that you spend more on interest, maintenance and renovations than you will get by way of return when you come to sell the property. Another risk is that if you can't pay the mortgage (for example if you lose your job) and are forced to sell at a time not of your choosing, you may make a loss.

When can I get my money back?

This investment class typically takes the longest time to convert to money as it takes time to prepare a property for sale and then 'put it on the market' and find a buyer for the price you want to sell it at. This process usually takes a few months and can take longer.

What return will I get?

With an investment property, the goal is to maximise both types of return: rental income and capital gain. The amount of your capital gain will depend on how much you bought the property for, how long you hold the property and then how strong the property market is when you come to sell.

If you live in the property, you won't be earning any income, unless you rent out a spare room. Unlike rent, the mortgage repayments are building your wealth by increasing ownership of your asset. But if you buy an investment property and rent it out, you will earn a regular income from your investment. The rate of return will depend on a number of factors: the type of property (commercial returns are usually higher than residential, but the risk is also higher), the supply and demand for that type of property and the demand for that area. Returns on investment properties vary from about 4% per annum for residential properties up to 20% for some types of commercial properties.

How complex is it?

The complexity involved in buying property is relatively high; it's the only form of investment where people routinely get a lawyer to act for them. There are different types of legal title (old system, torrens, strata, company, community, leasehold) and quite a few investigations to be made to ensure you're not buying a lemon, either structurally, with problems such as white ants, or legally, such as an undisclosed restriction on how you can use the property. This makes the transaction costs of buying real estate much higher than for other types of investments. Alternatively, you can invest in a managed property trust, where the trust manager takes care of the administration, though you will be paying fees to cover costs and services.

How is it taxed?

For investment properties, the rental income is included as part of your taxable income. The expenses you incur in earning that rental income, including property maintenance and the interest you pay on the money you borrowed to buy the property, can be claimed as tax deductions.

Like shares, investment properties (that is, a property you don't live in) are subject to capital gains tax if you own the property for more than one year. The laws on this have changed over time so it depends on when you bought your property and when you sell it.

The possibility of negative gearing often motivates people to choose property as an investment. If the expenses on the property are more than the rent you receive, the difference can be deducted from your other taxable income, such as your salary. This can be fine in the short term, but your long-term objective with any investment is to make a profit, not a loss.

What are my options?

You can choose to buy your own property to live in, a residential or commercial property to rent out, or invest in a managed property trust. Once you own a property you can consider using the equity you have in that property (i.e. the value of the property over and above what you owe on it) for borrowing money to invest for other purposes – so long as you can meet the repayments. Borrowing to invest using real estate as your security will get you the cheapest interest rates available.

3. Shares

People typically get interested in shares when there is a 'bull' (strong) market where seemingly everyone you talk to is making money buying and selling shares. This is not the time to start buying shares in the hope of wealth without work! Shares have the highest risk of the three classes, which is why it's worthwhile to spend some time to learn about them. Start an investment club, join up for some lectures at the stock exchange, read the finance section of the newspaper or a finance magazine or register for internet broking – it's free, so you can learn from the site before you start to buy and sell shares. If choosing which shares to buy is not for you, then you can still invest in this class by going through a professional fund manager.

Investing in shares will suit investors with different amounts of money to invest and accommodate different time frames. You can buy shares for the short, medium or long term, but generally you will make the biggest capital gain over a five to ten-year period or longer.

What are they?

Shares are units of ownership in a company that is listed on the stock exchange. They can be for an Australian or overseas company. Equity is another word used for shares; your shares are your equity (share of ownership) in the company.

How much do I need?

You need as little as $500 to begin investing in shares. Generally you would buy a 'parcel' of shares at a time, so you can start with one parcel as an initial investment, and buy more whenever you're ready.

What is the risk?

Share investment is the highest risk of the three classes. Companies do go bust and the shareholders lose all or most of their money

(HIH and One.Tel being examples). Share prices are very volatile – they can drop dramatically, and sometimes quickly go up in value during boom periods. People do make money on shares, and over the long term they tend to outperform the other investment classes. Remember, the higher the risk the higher the return.

There are a number of ways you can reduce the risks: one way is to research the company you are looking to invest in, and another is to spread your investments across different companies. Also, you can invest in a managed fund where professional fund managers spend their days doing this kind of analysis and using it to make investment decisions from the money pooled. See further on 'Should I invest directly or use a managed fund?'.

When can I get my money back?

You can sell all or just some of your shares at any time. You have to pay a brokerage fee each time you buy or sell.

What return will I get?

As with property, if you invest in shares you would expect to earn income (in the form of dividends), as well as making capital gains as the value of the shares increases. A *dividend* is a share of the profit the company earns. Dividends are usually paid out to the shareholders once or twice per year, though companies will not always pay a dividend. A *capital gain* is the difference between what you paid for the share and how much you sell the share for.

How complex are they?

You can buy shares directly. This has been made a whole lot easier in recent years as internet broking allows you to buy and sell shares for as little as $15 per transaction. When you buy a parcel of shares, you need to determine what your purpose is. Is it short-term – 'I heard they are going up so I want a quick profit' – or long-term – 'These shares are good growth shares and their value will go up over a 10-year period, so will be good for my retirement'? Your purpose will determine the complexity of your share investing. If you are investing for short-term gain you will need to monitor your shares closely to determine the best buying and selling times. But if you are investing for the long term you can relax more, knowing that your shares are likely to grow in value over the long term – though you should still monitor your investments.

Why not start an investment club as a way of learning about shares and not committing large sums of money while you learn? Our book, *The Money Club*, is an easy-to-read guide to starting an investment club.

You can also invest money into a managed fund where a professional fund manager will invest the pool of investors' money into a number of different shares. Managed funds will have different investment philosophies; for example, some will concentrate on dividends, some on growth potential, some will just mirror the index of the leading 200 Australian companies. See below for more details on the fees charged by managed funds.

How are shares taxed?

Returns from dividends and capital gains have to be included in your tax return as income.

Some dividends may have *franking credits* (some other terms you may have heard are *franked dividends* and *imputation credits*) attached to them. All this means is that the company is passing on a credit for the income tax they have already paid, for you to use to reduce your personal income tax. Let's say the company you have shares in made a profit of $100 and they pay tax of $30 (assuming the company tax rate is 30%). They then distribute a dividend of $10 to you. In your personal tax you will have income consisting of $10 dividends received but you will also have a credit of $3 towards tax to be paid by you – otherwise it would be double collecting by the Tax Office, from the company and from you.

You will have to pay capital gains tax on any profit you make when you sell your shares. The amount you need to declare will vary depending on how long you have held the shares.

What are my options?

Shares in different companies have different risk profiles; some are much riskier than others. How do you know which ones are the higher risk? Well, a new company that does not have a track record is considered more risky than an established company that has been performing well over a period of time. These established companies are sometimes called 'blue chip' shares but even these are not immune to bad performance. Blue chips such as AMP, Telstra and Coles Myer have lost value over the last few years. Australia has also had spectacular failures in some start-up companies such as One.Tel. Finally, there are defensive stocks that perform well and increase in value in most economic circumstances, such as Foodlands.

So what should you do? You put your eggs in many different baskets by buying shares in companies with different risk profiles in different sectors, because over a medium to long-term timeframe shares will always outperform putting your money in the bank.

Should I invest directly or use a managed fund?

Once you are comfortable with the different classes to invest in, you need to decide if your investment should be made directly or by using a managed fund. This is the difference between owning the shares or property outright, and buying into a shared investment with a whole lot of other people, managed by a professional fund manager. Remember, you can have a combination of both.

Managed funds are offered by professional fund management companies, banks and other financial institutions such as Colonial, ING, Westpac, ANZ, BT and NRMA. Look in the financial newspapers or magazines, or on websites such as www.morningstar. com.au, for lists of the types of funds you can buy into, plus comparison tables of their performance over various periods of time. Performance figures are usually calculated after ongoing fees and assuming income is re-invested – check the table source. Also look at the entry price (this is the amount you pay per unit) and the exit price (the amount you receive when you sell).

The usual way to invest in a managed fund is by unit trust. This means you buy a unit in a fund, which is managed under a trust deed. The manager pools the money and buys the category of investments that the fund is set up for. This could be cash, shares, property or various combinations of these.

The manager charges fees for making the investment decisions in accordance with the objectives of the fund (trust). They will decide where to invest, what portion and for how long. The fund's prospectus will tell you the aim of the fund, what it can invest in, how the money is allocated, the cost of the fund, how to invest, the legal structure, your rights and the risks associated with it. Always check what a fund's published performance (or return) has been over a period of time before making your decision, and check what fees you will pay.

There can be four different types of fees (these come from an excellent article by *Choice Magazine*, 'Take the puzzle out of investing', February 2002, p. 12):

1. *Entry fee*: Up-front fee (up to 5% of your investment) charged on your initial amount invested and any amounts added after that.
2. *Exit fee*: Percentage fees some funds charge when you leave.
3. *Management expense ratio (MER)*: Ongoing fees, expressed as a percentage of the total funds under management, and usually ranging from 0.8% to 2.4%. They include the manager's fee, the trailing commission to your financial adviser (see next point) and other fees such as audit fees.
4. *Trail*: Ongoing commission to the adviser or discount broker who introduced you to the fund. It's included in the MER and usually ranges from 0.3% to 0.6%. On top of the trail some financial advisers charge an *adviser service fee* for ongoing service.

You are or can be an investor! You have gone through the basics of investing, answered some questions about yourself and now can look for particular features to choose from in the three investment classes that will suit your style and personal situation. As Danielle said, educate yourself and just start! In our next chapter on building wealth we hear from people who did just that with great results.

CHAPTER 7

Growing and building your wealth

Building wealth is not about building up the dollars in your bank account. Building wealth is aimed at owning assets that will produce a passive income. This is not the same thing as being wealthy or rich. It's about gaining an income from your investment assets, so you're not always dependent on earning an income.

There are piles of books, articles and even websites about how to get rich quickly, but unfortunately there is no such thing. Unless they have inherited their money, anyone who has built up wealth has done it through hard work and calculated decisions.

In this chapter we are not giving you financial advice. What we aim to do is go through a number of ways and options to build wealth. We also give examples of some of the things we have done. Some of our decisions have been good ones and are paying off and others have not – being financially fit means taking risks, knowing that not all of your investments will pay off but that through wise decision-making you can maximise the good decisions and minimise the bad ones.

How to build your wealth

There are numerous ways of building your wealth. You could start a business or build up an existing one, which could then be managed by someone else to provide you with an ongoing income. Or you could buy an asset, for example an investment property, which you pay off over time and which will eventually provide you with capital growth, some tax advantages and an income in the form of rent. There are many different ways to fund these activities, for example through a bank loan, a loan against the equity in your home, or a margin loan.

Building wealth requires an understanding of your own position and financial goals. Having the right ideas, advice and information is also important. Talk to friends and relatives and find yourself a financial adviser that you feel comfortable with to help you. Finding the right adviser can be the best investment you make. We talk about this more in Chapter 8.

Developing your knowledge and getting guidance

Developing your knowledge is vital. We did it gradually over time, gaining confidence slowly. We helped each other by sharing information. You need to be able to make informed and in most cases good decisions as well as differentiate good advice from bad. There are lots of places to start – such as reading the investment sections of the newspaper, looking at the stock exchange books and website, and looking at books from the Financial Planning Association. You can also subscribe to magazines and bulletins distributed by financial planners, consulting firms, investment banks and so on. These are informative and usually free.

Some people work through and develop personal wealth plans. These plans involve setting goals. If you are going to do this the goals need to be specific as well as realistic, and include timeframes and plans which can also give you flexibility as circumstances might change.

Your net worth

Wealth creation is about increasing what is sometimes called your *net worth*. Net worth can be described as:

$$Assets - Liabilities = Net\ Worth$$

A wealth creation *asset* is a possession that generates income or provides a return, such as:

- A savings account
- A retirement plan
- Shares and bonds
- A house

Some possessions (like your car, lounge suite, big screen TV or DVD player) are assets, but they aren't wealth-creating assets because they don't earn money or rise in value.

A *liability*, also called a debt, is money you owe, such as:

- A car loan
- Your mortgage
- Credit card balances
- Personal loans

How to work out your net worth

Your net worth is the difference between your assets and liabilities. Net worth is your wealth.

By filling in the following worksheet you will start to get some idea of your net worth.

ASSETS	Current value $
Personal assets	
Family home or unit	
Contents of home	
Motor vehicles	
Caravan, boat, other leisure assets	
Jewellery	
Holiday home	
Art, antiques and collectables	
Other personal assets	

ASSETS *(continued)*	Current value $
Cash on hand	
TOTAL	$............
Cash assets	
Savings and cheque accounts	
Short-term deposits	
Cash management accounts	
Credit union and building society accounts	
Other	
TOTAL	$............
Investment assets	
Bonds	
Warrants/options	
Shares	
Real estate	
Managed funds/unit trusts	
Insurance/friendly society bonds	
Other	
Superannuation (not accessible until you are 55–60)	
Allocated pensions/annuities	
Other superannuation pensions	
Other	
TOTAL	$............
TOTAL ASSETS	$............

LIABILITIES	Current value $
Personal debt	
Car loan	
Home mortgage	
Overdraft	
Money owed	
TOTAL	$............

LIABILITIES *(continued)*	Current value $
Short-term debt and committed expenditure	
Credit card debts	
Income tax owing	
Any other liabilities	
TOTAL	$............
Investment debt	
Investment loans	
Margin loan	
Overdraft	
Other	
TOTAL	$............
TOTAL LIABILITIES	$............
NET WEALTH (total assets – total liabilities) =	

Gearing

Gearing is the term used to describe borrowing in order to buy an income-producing asset. There are great potential tax advantages to taking out a loan to fund an investment. This is because the interest repayments on your investment are tax deductible – whereas the interest on your home loan is not.

Negative gearing

Negative gearing occurs when the cost of borrowing is greater than the income produced. In a tax context, negative gearing means off-setting losses (i.e. when the income from an investment property or shares is less than the expenses, including the interest repayments) against your other assessable and taxable income. When this occurs, as long as particular criteria are met, then a tax deduction can be made, which is often used to reduce your overall tax bill.

The most common example of negative gearing occurs in the property and share markets. What usually happens is that an investor borrows money to acquire property or shares. In most cases, the interest on the borrowings will be deductible if the money was borrowed to acquire an income-producing asset, such as a rent-producing property.

Negative gearing is one way that people use to assist them to build up their assets, because the loss, which has to be made up from your cashflow every month, is partly offset by being deductible against your other income.

There are many things to consider before you enter into negative gearing arrangements. Having a financial adviser is important so that you can discuss your individual circumstances and plans and whether negative gearing would work for you. Things which you may need to consider before thinking about negative gearing include:

- Do you have equity in your home or other assets? The more equity you have, the easier it will be to borrow money to fund another investment at home loan rates of interest.
- Do you have a steady income? As negative gearing essentially involves incurring a loss every month, you will need a secure income from another source to make up the difference.
- Is your taxable income in the highest income bracket? The tax benefits of negative gearing correlate to your marginal rate of tax. The higher your marginal rate, the greater the benefit from negative gearing.

Over time, as the income from your investment increases, the loss you make will become smaller and smaller and will eventually turn into a profit. This is the aim of any investment; even though you lose the tax deduction, overall you are much better off.

Positive gearing

Where an asset such as a property earns *more* income than the expenses or deductions, this is referred to as 'positive gearing'. A property will be geared 'positively' if the rental income equals or exceeds the deductible expenses (such as interest payments, rates and land tax associated with that property).

There is therefore no tax deduction which can be made against your other income. However, you are still benefiting from the leverage that comes from gearing. Compared to buying the asset outright, in the short term you won't receive as much, if any, return, because the rent or dividends will go to pay off the loan. In the longer term, though, your capital gain will be higher. For example, if you have $100,000 to invest, and values double, when you sell you will receive $200,000 and your capital gain will be approximately $100,000. But if you borrowed an extra $100,000 to buy a $200,000 asset, when you sell you will receive $400,000, so your capital gain has also doubled to $200,000.

Funding options – borrowing money

There is a great deal of information on various types of loans, interest rates, loan periods and so on. There are whole magazines devoted just to mortgages. There are sections in most newspapers, websites and even mortgage brokers who will help you compare different banks and lending institutions.

The security you have will usually determine how much money you can borrow and what rate you can get. Most people start by paying off all or part of the mortgage on their home and using this equity as security to borrow money to put into an investment. Property is the form of security most favoured by lenders, and with this type of security the interest rate will be lower. Shares can also be used as security, with the interest rate dependent on how safe the company is perceived to be.

Margin loans

Margin lending is where an individual borrows money to invest in shares and build wealth. The actual shares are used as security against the loan and then the borrowed amount helps the investor buy more shares with the view of increasing his or her return.

This is another example of leveraging or gearing. The idea here is that the value of your portfolio will grow at a greater rate than the cost of borrowing. This works if the portfolio value goes up – however, if the value goes down the value of security declines and the value of your portfolio also declines.

Here is an example of how a marginal loan might work. If you had $30,000 saved, you might want to build a portfolio of shares using a margin loan. Depending on the shares you buy, you can usually borrow up to 70% of the value of the share portfolio, so you could buy a portfolio valued at $100,000. If the market rises by 10%, you have made a capital gain of $10,000, rather than the gain of $3,000 if you had only invested the $30,000 of your own.

If the market falls, of course, your loss is correspondingly greater, and the lender may make a 'margin call'; you would have to sell shares or pay cash to keep the loan ratio at 70%. So for example if the market fell by 10%, you would have to pay the lender $7,000 because the limit of what you can owe has dropped from $70,000 to $63,000.

Acquiring investment assets – our stories

Buying property

Frances recounts her experience when she and Emily bought an investment unit together.

For a while I had been thinking about buying an investment property, but was put off by the low rental returns from residential properties in my local area. Rents were usually about 4%–5%, before deducting expenses such as management fees, rates, and interest on the loan. We were going to borrow the whole amount, and I didn't want to have to meet a large gap in cashflow every month.

Then I saw an ad in the paper for a new development in the Port Stephens area; a resort development where you could own a strata apartment and have it managed as a serviced unit in the resort. I mentioned this to Emily, and she'd seen the same ad and was interested too. We went up for a day with our families to look at the display centre (the property was just a hole in the ground at that stage) and had a very nice lunch with our kids on the waterfront. The development looked great, but we were feeling cautious, and decided to go halves and buy a unit together.

We had a choice of one or two bedroom units; we decided to go for a one bedroom unit, because we thought it would be likely to have a higher rate of occupancy, and because the two bedroom units either had no view, or were much more expensive.

We were just in time to choose the last one bedroom unit in the development, and settled back to wait the next 18 months while the building went up. When it was time to settle, we had quite a drama: our unit was one of only two in the whole complex without a spa – instead it had an open shower to cater for disabled people. This was a huge problem – the spa had been a major selling point for us. Legally we were in the right; the contract said that the spa was included. The agent had made a mistake. He tried to talk us into going ahead anyway, but we did a bit of research with other properties in the area and were advised that during low periods, a unit without a spa would always be the last to be let out.

After much anguish, the problem was solved; another purchaser had failed to complete their purchase, and we could have their unit instead. So the deal went ahead. Emily and I had an agreement drawn up to work out when we could use the unit ourselves, and what will happen if one of us wants to sell.

We've owned the unit for 18 months now. As it is in a brand new building, and the purchase price included all the furniture, we can get a tax deduction for depreciation. This means that the investment is slightly cashflow positive – the money we receive, including the depreciation, is just a little more than the expenses, including interest on the loan. We don't have to pay any more out of our own pockets, although the income dips up and down wildly during the year, depending on the season.

We're happy with our investment, and it's worth quite a bit more now than what we paid for it.

The things Frances and Emily have learnt from this experience are:

- Make sure the contract sets out exactly what you expect to be getting.
- Do as much research as you can into factors likely to affect the tenancy of the property. Who will rent it out? What demographic does it appeal to? Is there any competition nearby? (The resort Frances and Emily's unit is in is the only one of its kind in the area.)
- Watch out for projected income figures from the agent. Although Frances and Emily are happy enough with the return

they are getting, the agent's projections were very optimistic. Make sure your investment would be sound even if the projected income isn't as large as expected.

• Going in with a friend may be a good way to buy a property you otherwise couldn't afford, but it's essential to have an agreement prepared to cover every aspect of joint ownership.

Emily has invested in other properties, too. Here is her story.

Although I had dabbled in the stock market, the amount of money I had invested was relatively small. I certainly hadn't thought of it in terms of real wealth creation. Things really changed after I was retrenched.

My husband and I work in the advertising industry, which is a precarious industry at the best of times. After having been through one retrenchment, I was determined that if it ever happened again, I would be financially covered. With both of us in the same industry, our concerns were twofold.

What was surprising, in my quest to secure a financial future, was that once I got started, things really took off. I'd done some research into purchasing an investment property. I attended seminars and kept up to date with recent sales in my area of interest, finally settling on a small studio in the inner city. The building and the unit had recently been renovated, the location was great and there were plenty of cafes and restaurants nearby. I remember feeling a huge relief, because we'd actually done it.

Generally, banks have been generous in lending for investment properties. Due to the fact that we had enough equity in our home loan, the bank agreed to lend us the money. Around this time, I also started to take share trading more seriously. With the advent of internet share trading, I was hooked. Not long after this I went on to start our investment club.

A year later, while visiting Melbourne, I was amazed at how cheap the prices of the units were compared with Sydney. So after a little investigation and one weekend trip to Melbourne (spent visiting a dozen units in one morning!) I bought another investment unit. For me this has been my best investment yet. The trick is to find a place that you consider has been overlooked, yet is full of potential. Our Melbourne investment unit has way surpassed the first one we bought, in terms of capital gains. I guess we were still learning with the first one.

Then Frances and I bought a small unit at Port Stephens on the New South Wales coast. Our unit is in a resort complex. Sharing the costs of this unit has given me exposure to another investment area that I could not have afforded on my own.

In a relatively short space of time I had acquired three investment units, although individually each was small. This proved that a person or couple on an average salary could do it. What I learnt was you don't have to have lots of money, as long as you have enough equity in your home. Then you have the opportunity to use this to your advantage and negatively gear your investments. I felt comfortable buying investment properties as a way to build wealth. Of course, you must follow a few simple rules. My number one rule is to research and do your homework well before you buy.

Recently, due to a change in our financial position, we had to sell the first unit we bought. We were incurring huge strata fees over a two-year period. While the building had undergone major renovations five years earlier, there was some structural damage that needed further repair, resulting in a considerable cost to the owners of the units. Also, the body corporate was having problems with the strata management. We decided that it was time to sell. In the five years we owned the unit, there were only three weeks when it was not occupied. I thought I'd done my homework and found a suitable location that would stay rented – and I was right, but I didn't anticipate the huge, ongoing repair costs on a newly renovated building.

Another thing we discovered, when we came to exchange with the new owner, was that our Certificate of Title on the unit had been misplaced. After much anxious searching, we uncovered the title somewhere deep in the archives of the bank that originally lent us the money to purchase. The search to find the Certificate of Title set us back three weeks and we nearly lost the sale. It's really important to keep track of paperwork!

Emily is still fond of using property as a way to build wealth, but there are some simple rules to follow:

- When buying a unit ask yourself a few questions:
  - Could I live in this area/unit? If you answer yes, then you have a better chance of getting tenants.
  - Is the infrastructure sufficient? For instance, is it close to public transport, supermarkets, cafes and parks?
  - Are there units in the area that are not being leased, or that have been without tenants for a long period?
- If you are buying a unit in a large block, check the quarterly strata management fees. If the fees are too high, they can negate any rental earnings you receive.
- Keep track of all the necessary paperwork.

Buying shares

We started our investment club, Sheba Investment Network (SIN), to help us learn about buying and selling shares. Earlier at one of our book club meetings we started talking about the stock market. We all admitted that we found the share market complex and confusing. Although we all worked and some of us had professional qualifications, we had not invested any money in shares. Understanding the stock market and what to buy and when to sell seemed daunting. That's when we decided to form an investment club. As a group we thought that it would be one way to find out information about the stock market and to start investing. Once we started meeting regularly, we all started learning a great deal and gaining confidence. We formed a partnership and started buying shares. We learnt a lot and had a great deal of fun – and our investments have always performed better than some of the professional managed funds. We still meet once a month and have now moved on to investing in other areas and using the same way of sharing information to help each other.

Since starting our investment club, all of us have started our own investment portfolios outside the club.

Dianne has bought shares through her self-managed super-annuation fund. Here's how she did it.

When I was four months pregnant with my daughter I decided to set up my own business as I knew it would be difficult to maintain the corporate life and long work days I had. This was made easier by the fact that my partner had a regular and secure income stream. I wanted time to be a mum but also time to work. So, with an ever-increasing belly size I found my first client and assignment. Over 10 years my partner and I built up the business plus I had the advantage of flexibility to be with my daughter. During this time, I only made the minimum superannuation guarantee payments. After a couple of good years, I decided we should start our own superannuation fund. This was initially driven by tax considerations but also the fact that at the age of 40 I had very little superannuation. Little did I know how valuable my superannuation fund would become in my financial education and what an important part of my retirement planning it would become, especially after my partner and I separated.

To get started, I went to my accountant armed with my personal and company information, and we went through the pros and cons of setting up a fund, how much it would cost and how much time and administration it would take.

Basically it will suit you if you earn a medium to high salary, you want to make your own investment decisions and you are prepared to spend time on your investments and on the paperwork and administration of the fund. I bought a standard trust deed, which is like buying a shelf company. These are usually around $600 to $1000. I set up the bank account and then transferred my existing 'managed' super fund money into my superannuation fund. The accountant applied for a Tax File Number (TFN) for the fund from the Australian Tax Office.

There is no point setting up your own fund unless you are prepared to do it properly, because in addition to being bound by the trust deed you are subject to the laws of the Superannuation Industry (Supervision) Act 1993 *plus the taxation laws. The trustee is like a company director and must act honestly in all matters; exercise the same degree of care, skill and diligence as an ordinary prudent person; act in the best interest of the fund members; keep the assets of the fund separate from other (personal) assets; and ensure that the monies cannot be used for any reason whatsoever and cannot be accessed until retirement (55 in my case).*

There is a lot of paperwork! I do my own 'accounting' as well as the investing decisions. The accountant does the year-end final accounts, tax return, audit and regular reporting, which costs a reasonable amount – mine was around $1500. I have transferred my life insurance policy to the super fund so the fee is paid by the fund. You need to work out what your contributions are and what the maximum amount is that you can contribute for your age group otherwise you will be subject to a surcharge tax if you exceed these contribution levels. You can only have a maximum of four members in a self-managed fund.

The best part has been making my own investment decisions. Being a member of an investment club has been a huge help for me as I get the collective input of our club, which I can then use in my own fund. My investing so far has been in buying Australian shares, plus I bought into a managed international fund and have recently branched out into investing in Aboriginal artworks.

An unexpected bonus has been the eduction flow-on effect to my daughter, who is 12 – she is now interested in what shares we buy.

Buying commercial property

Di recently went to see her financial adviser and was extremely interested in his approach to investing in commercial property.

I had never even considered commercial property as a potential place to invest because of the high entry cost. My financial adviser was chatting to me about how some of his clients were grouping together to make it possible for them to invest in commercial buildings such as office blocks. These office buildings, once assessed for income-generating potential as well as capital growth, would be offered and bought by a small group of investors. They pool their resources and invest in the building together. They have completed a number of these group buys and the buildings are returning currently around 10% in rental – and of course over the longer term they, should produce capital growth for the owners. I am now looking at investing in a share of a commercial building as this is a different sector from the residential property market and should provide me with some diversification. As a small investor I had never even looked at commercial property as I thought that it was outside my financial capability.

Superannuation

This book would not be complete if we did not touch on super-annuation as another way to build wealth for the future. Think of it as part of your training to become financially fit. It's like feeding your body with nutrients in your younger years to keep you in shape as you get older. The same can be said of superannuation. The money you put away while you're working will be your buffer to support you when you need it most.

Why do we need superannuation? Because the Australian government cannot guarantee a pension for all Australians. The fact is, we are living longer. As an ageing population there will not be enough to go around. We have to accept that the government pension in its current form may no longer exist when most of us retire. Increasingly, people will be forced to rely upon their super-annuation as their only source of retirement income.

Now, before the muscles in your neck tense up, we'll attempt to make the topic of superannuation as easy as possible to digest. Superannuation is not a subject to take lightly, so please seek professional advice, particularly if you are in the midst of changing your fund or are approaching retirement age.

Superannuation is another form of investing in the three asset classes we looked at in the previous chapter. Superannuation funds invest in a mix of cash, shares and property. 'Super' is just a type of investment structure that stops you accessing your funds until you retire, and has a different tax treatment to normal investments. In addition, your super is taxed differently depending what stage it is at: when it is invested, while it produces earnings and when it is cashed in.

Superannuation will be the foundation of your savings for your future or retirement. Simply, this will be the money that has been squirrelled away from your wages and invested solely for the purpose of providing you with enough to live off once you have retired from the workforce.

The benefit of superannuation is that it is a forced saving. If you work for an employer (as opposed to being self-employed), by law your employer must take out a percentage of your salary and invest this into a super fund. Currently the compulsory superannuation guarantee contribution is at 9%. These days, most superannuation funds have a number of investment options, from which you or your employer can choose to have your superannuation money invested in.

The principle of taking money out before it lands into your wallet is a major plus, as you really don't miss it. For those who have a hard time saving, superannuation may be all they have when they retire.

Superannuation funds with investment choices are similar to managed funds but with different tax structures. There are generally more tax concessions involved when money is invested in the superannuation environment. Saving tax in any form is a big plus, and therefore another benefit of superannuation. If you have any tax-related queries you can contact the Australian Taxation Office's superannuation helpline on 13 10 20. Another helpful website is the Australian Consumer Association at www.choice.com.au.

Whether your superannuation money is invested in a fund of your choice or not, you should find out about the investment returns that you have earned on your superannuation money. Remember that superannuation is a long-term investment and is your designated retirement nest egg, so you should make sure that you are happy with the amount of earnings your superannuation money is achieving.

Depending on your age and the length of time you have been in the workforce, the amount you have invested in super over the years may or may not be enough for your retirement. What exactly is 'enough'? Most experts believe you should aim for an annual retirement income of around 65% of your current income.

If you begin contributing to super in your early twenties, and are continuously employed until retirement at 65, by the time you retire you should have enough to live on just from the compulsory 9% surcharge. This is based on your regular contributions going into a super fund earning around 5% or 6% on average over the period of your working life. For a more accurate projection you should speak to your financial planner or superannuation fund manager.

Let's say you have left it too late and you begin contributing into a super fund in your forties. To reap the same benefits as someone who had started their contribution in their early twenties, you will have to contribute twice as much into your fund. This means putting in extra voluntary contributions, on top of the 9% minimum. If you can persuade your employer to 'salary sacrifice', these payments can come out of your gross income, and you won't have to pay income tax on them, just the (lower) superannuation contribution tax. If you are thinking of putting this off until you are older, or earning more, think again as this could be detrimental, especially as the job market for older people is uncertain. The point here is to start sooner rather than later. Remember that the principle of compounding returns means that if you put in more earlier, you will earn *much* more later.

Depending on the superannuation fund your money has been invested in, you can nominate to take your benefit as an allocated pension, a lump sum, or a combination of both. There are often benefits in choosing to take at least part of your benefit as a pension, especially if you fear you might spend your lump sum payout in one hit.

As well, if you take a lump sum payout you will have to pay tax on this amount. If you roll your super into an allocated pension, you won't have to pay the lump sum tax. This means you'll have more money in your pocket and more capital on which to keep earning interest.

You should speak to a financial adviser when you are approaching retirement to discuss the tax implications, along with the best form of payment, to suit your needs.

Tips to keep track of your superannuation

- Make sure you know the name of the superannuation fund that your employer pays your contribution to. Also, check that it is reputable. Once again, you can refer to the Australian Tax Office helpline (13 10 20). You may have to press a few buttons before you get onto an adviser, but it will be worth the wait.
- Check your contribution statements. Go through these with a fine-toothed comb, especially as these statements usually only come once a year. Make a note of the earnings on your superannuation fund and assess whether you feel they are adequate. Your fund should be giving you a similar rate of return to a managed fund investing in the same

types of assets. Ring your super fund and have them explain anything you do not understand on your statement. Remember, you are entitled to ask as many questions as you need to.

- If you have a number of super funds, consolidate them into the current one. It is very confusing to keep track of small amounts invested in various super funds, especially if you move in and out of jobs. This will also save on the fees charged by each fund that eat into your contributions.
- Don't put all your eggs in one basket. Make sure your fund offers a diversified range of investments; for example, it should invest in bonds and property trusts as well as shares.

How can I tell if I have enough super?

Financial planners can do the projections. It depends on many factors, including whether you own your own home and what level of income you will need to satisfy your lifestyle requirements when you retire.

There are websites with easy-to-use calculators, such as www. investmentwarehouse.com.au. The calculator allows you to work out how much you will need to contribute, based on your current income. This will help establish how much you will need in retirement.

The figures below give you an indication of how much of a lump sum you will need to generate various annual incomes during retirement. This is calculated on a lump sum superannuation payout earning around 6% to 7% per annum:

- $330,000 will generate $20,000
- $480,000 will generate $30,000
- $820,000 will generate $50,000
- $1,000,000 will generate $60,000

Which investment option offered by my super fund is best for me?

As a general rule, the closer you are to retirement, the more conservative your investment choice will be. The younger you are, the higher-risk/higher-growth investments you can choose. This is because over a 10-year-plus period, most investments such as shares will increase. During this time period, in the shorter term, they might go down, before they go up again.

What is a do-it-yourself (DIY) super fund?

Instead of paying their super contributions to a financial institution, some people set up their own superannuation fund, as Dianne has done. They have a deed drawn up, appointing their company or themselves as trustee of the fund, and they have to comply with a whole host of regulations to make sure that their fund invests in the right type of investment and doesn't pay anything out to the members until they have retired.

The advantages of having your own super fund are:

- You have more control over management fees.
- You can control exactly what your superannuation funds are invested in.

The disadvantages of having your own fund are:

- The costs of running the fund and complying with the ever-changing regulations are high – generally it's not considered worthwhile for an initial investment of less than $100,000.
- It's a lot more effort than just handing the money over to a professional manager and letting them do all the work. You really have to know what you are doing.

Your attitude towards superannuation will depend very much on how old you are. If you are in your twenties, it's not too exciting to concentrate on a form of investment that you can't get your hands on for another 35 to 40 years. Fair enough – most people in their twenties want to enjoy the freedom that money gives them once they start working. Yet it's the contributions you make when you are young that will pay off in the long term due to the effect of compounding. As you get closer to retirement age, it's amazing how your level of interest in your super fund will grow every year.

Retirement

Retirement should be like the pot of gold at the end of the rainbow. The years of routine are behind, and you can start to focus on the things you have always wanted to do. By now, the mortgage on your home is paid off, the children are off your hands, and your work commitments no longer hold you back.

Sound too good to be true? Well, with careful planning you can achieve these goals. Retirement should be a time for you to enjoy your life and focus on achieving your long-term goals – whether it is the holiday you've always wanted, or time to spend on your favourite sporting activity, such as golf or tennis. Or you could try something new like yoga. For those who still need the challenge of working, you might look for a part-time work or even start your own business. Some simply long for the day when they can spend time with their partner, children, grandchildren and friends.

Why do I need to plan for retirement?

Planning ahead is crucial for any couple or single person looking for a comfortable living standard in their retirement. After all, you could have as much as twenty to thirty years left for retirement. This is a long time in any language not to have a plan of action. Remember that retirement is from the work force, *not from life*.

If you are unsure of how much money you will need to comfortably live on, then completing your Money Picture in Chapter 3 will help you identify where you spend your money and how much you will need to maintain a comfortable lifestyle. A retirement strategy is just another part of your overall plan to become financially fit. If you put into action the principles discussed in this book, then you will have enough of a nest egg in place to see you through these years.

Elizabeth is 64 years old and single, and manages to combine part-time work and a busy social life. She receives a regular pension from her superannuation.

I've been retired for nine years now. I took my super in the form of a pension, so I always knew how much money I'd have to live on; it's calculated as a proportion of my previous salary.

I'm doing some casual work one or two days a week and I appreciate the extra money it brings in. All my retired friends are doing this, because they've found that they're spending more than they were when they were working.

Being retired is an expensive lifestyle, because there are so many more opportunities to spend – for example, travel and meeting friends for lunch. In theory, I should be spending less on some things, such as clothes, but in reality I don't.

I've used my retirement to do some new things. For example, I've learnt how to use the internet and bought a computer. I've got much more time for exercise than when I was working – walking and Pilates. The majority of people in my Pilates class are in their sixties or seventies!

Surprisingly, about 80% of retirees are living on $20,000 a year or less. This is a small amount, although bear in mind that most have paid off their homes and their children are no longer living with them.

The average age for retirement is around 60 to 65. By today's standards this is not old at all. Depending on your date of birth (there is a sliding scale for people born between 1960 and 1965), once you've retired you will be eligible to access your superannuation. Based on your financial lifestyle requirements, you will have to decide whether to take a lump sum payout or an allocated pension.

Don't leave it too late to plan for your retirement – the sooner you start, the better. There is no escaping the challenges that lie ahead, but once you become financially fit then the money issues won't be a problem. Maintaining a healthy mind, body and bank account are the key.

Tips if you are approaching retirement

- Start planning for your retirement. Set up social networks, join local clubs, do volunteer work or go back to study.
- Keep healthy, mentally and physically.
- Physically, have an exercise program in place. Not too strenuous, but a gentle exercise routine. Form or join a walking club.
- Challenge yourself; try something you would never have done before.

- You may be eligible for discounts on water rates, council rates, telephone and car registrations.
- Movie and theatre tickets are also discounted.
- Make the most of reduced transport costs. A concession travel card is available.

Finding and sharing information

We have found that our investment club has given us a good forum for our group to discuss and share information on a whole range of investments. We have also spent a number of evenings giving our own accounts of what we have tried to do, who we got advice from, where we borrowed money and at what rate. We have also invested in things together to cut down our risk and personal exposure. As we find out new information or approaches we usually share this with the group, and it adds significantly to our group knowledge. Rules and regulations, as well as options, prices and potential, change regularly so it is good to keep track of things. We even ask financial advisers or experts in a particular area to come to our meetings and share their ideas.

Once you have money to invest and have set your sights on a particular goal, then building wealth is about time and focus. When you are building wealth, you are really reaping the rewards of financial fitness. It's very satisfying to watch the value of your investment assets increase over time, giving you diverse sources of income other than your salary, and more choices in your life. To get the most out of your investment assets you'll need some expert advice. In the next chapter we look at how to go about finding the best people to be on your support team.

CHAPTER 8

Getting help – choosing an accountant, financial planner and lawyer

Accountants, financial planners and lawyers should all have a place in your support team. Before you dive in, work out what you need from them, then find an adviser who you feel comfortable with.

Everyone needs professional advice from time to time. It's like having a support team for your financial fitness. That's not to say you shouldn't learn about legal issues, tax and financial planning, but professionals in these fields spend years studying, followed by more years of experience in their jobs. They will bring information to the table that you just don't have. The money you spend on professional advice will be a lot less than the money you risk losing by acting without advice. Think of it as an investment in yourself.

Having said that, of course, it's still crucial to choose the right people to be on your team. There are lots of professional advisers around. Choosing the wrong one can be disastrous. Choosing the right one will not just give you a great financial outcome, but will increase your confidence in your own skills and decision-making abilities.

So how do you find the right people? As a general rule, word of mouth is worth paying attention to, but you should take other factors into account. What works for friends or relatives won't necessarily work for you. The person giving the recommendation might have had quite a different problem to yours, and the adviser's field of expertise might have been right for them, but not for you.

There are two aspects to finding the right adviser. First, they have to have the right technical expertise. This comes down to a combination of formal qualifications and experience. Second, you have to feel comfortable with them. The personal relationship is just as important as the technical aspects. This is the person to whom you'll be revealing all your financial secrets, and you might be tempted not to tell the whole story if you feel that the adviser will criticise or demean you.

Don't forget that *you* are the client and are paying the bills; if you're not comfortable with the advice or services you're getting, or if you feel that your adviser is not listening to you or taking you seriously, you don't have to put up with them. Don't be afraid to get a second opinion and/or change advisers.

Finding an accountant

What can an accountant do for me?

The first contact most of us have with an accountant is to get our tax return done; because we want to make sure that it's done properly, and because we rely on our accountant to have detailed and up-to-date knowledge of taxation. An accountant's knowledge of tax is not just helpful at tax time; accountants can also give tax advice when you are thinking about investing (for example, in whose name should the investment be held?) and when you are making your will (for example, what are the tax consequences for your beneficiaries?).

If you are self-employed, or have to lodge Business Activity Statements (BAS), your accountant can also help you set up systems to comply with the various record-keeping and reporting requirements. Accountants can also give you management advice for your business, eg evaluating a business before you buy it, or helping you prepare a business plan.

Some accountants are also licensed investment advisers, and can therefore give investment advice as well.

Choosing an accountant

Word of mouth is quite often the best way to find out about a 'good accountant', but you need to take into account what service you want and match it to the accountant you choose. Dianne Hill, who is the accountant amongst us, gets asked regularly to recommend an accountant. The first thing she asks is, what do you want your accountant to do for you? Define your needs up-front – not when you are sitting in front of the accountant and paying per hour for their time. What do you want and where do you want to go?

Be aware that anyone can call himself or herself an accountant. We suggest the first question you ask the accountant is what his or her qualifications and experience are and what professional association he or she belongs to.

There are three professional bodies for accountants in Australia: the Institute of Chartered Accountants in Australia (www.icaa. org.au), the Australian Society of Certified Public Accountants (www.cpaaustralia.org.au), and the National Institute of Accountants (www.nia.org.au). Members of the first two must have completed at least a prescribed university degree, an entry course, and have specific work experience. Members of the NIA need to have completed a diploma in accounting, plus work experience.

In addition to membership of any of the above bodies, if your accountant is preparing your tax return, he or she must also be a registered tax agent.

Am I better off with a small suburban firm or a large city firm?

The advantages and disadvantages listed below apply equally to accountants and lawyers.

The advantages of going to a small firm are:

- Usually lower fees
- A more personal level of service
- Often a more convenient suburban location

The advantages of seeing an accountant or lawyer in a larger firm are:

- Others can take over if your lawyer or accountant is sick or away on holidays.

- Often they provide a higher degree of specialisation and expertise (again, check back to what your needs are).
- Access to others in the firm for advice if your case strays into a number of different areas of law or accounting.

Is there any way I can save on fees?

Accountants charge by the hour. The more legwork you can do yourself, the more you will save in fees. Discuss the following suggestions with your accountant:

- Organise all your information, especially expenses. You could put all your expenses into a spreadsheet or set up a filing system where you can come home and put dockets out of your wallet into different folders or trays that you have labelled.
- Ask the accountant what cost codes they use in their accounting package – for example, code number 1234 = travel expenses. You can set this up to match on your spreadsheet and reduce the amount of processing time by staff in the accountant's office.
- Get all your documentation, bank statements, credit card statements, pay slips, group certificates, receipts etc together (an easy way to do this as you go is to go to the stationery shop and get a tray or folder; mark the folder 'tax deductible expenses'). Ask your accountant what you should be collecting, e.g. uniform expenses, study costs, etc. Whatever your system, make it easy for you to keep documents together – that way you are not paying for someone else to do it for you.
- You can go back to last year's tax return and look at the categories of income and expenses to give you a starting point even before going to see an accountant.

Finding a financial planner

What can a financial planner do for me?

Financial planners give investment advice, and carry out the mechanics of investing your money on your behalf; that is, they take the money that you have available to invest and pay it into whatever investment you have agreed on. They will often handle the ongoing paperwork involved and carry out regular reviews of your investment portfolio. An adviser should be able to advise you on both wealth creation and retirement planning. A financial planner will have some knowledge of tax, but he or she should encourage you to check your tax situation separately with your accountant.

Choosing a financial planner

It is absolutely critical that you only deal with an adviser who is properly licensed. In March 2002 a new financial services law came into operation. This law states that anyone who provides advice in relation to financial products must be licensed. Plus, before you decide which financial product to invest in, the adviser must give you:

- A Financial Services Guide
- A Statement of Advice, and
- A Product Disclosure Statement

The new law sets up a dispute resolution scheme and, for some types of products, you will be entitled to a cooling-off period of 14 days after you sign up.

The purpose of the new law is to improve the quality of advice given by financial planners, by making sure that they have the appropriate formal qualifications, and to improve disclosure of the costs involved. If your adviser is not aware of these laws, or doesn't give you the documents required, walk straight out the door.

Broadly speaking, there are two types of adviser: those linked to a financial institution, and those who are independent. Although the advisers linked to a financial institution, such as a bank, may present their services as 'free', this is not really the case. These advisers receive a commission from the institutions that run the products they recommend. The commission paid to the adviser is taken out of your investment. The new licensing regulations should help make it clear how much commission the adviser will receive. Some independent advisers will also charge on a commission basis; it's not limited to the in-house advisers.

The alternative method of charging is by reference to an agreed fee, usually based on an hourly rate. This can seem more painful to the client, as you are directly writing a cheque to the adviser. However, these advisers will refund any commission they receive back to the consumer. Therefore, an adviser charging on this basis will have no incentive to recommend one investment over another one that doesn't pay as big a commission.

Whatever fee structure you agree on, make sure that it's properly disclosed to you at the outset and that you understand exactly how much the whole process, including regular reviews, will cost.

You may have heard of a study conducted by the Australian Securities and Investments Commission (ASIC) and the Australian Consumers Association (ACA) into the financial planning industry, reported in February 2003. Fifty-three genuine consumers, acting as 'shadow shoppers', were sent out to a wide variety of advisers asking for an investment plan. Overall, the study found a poor level of investment advice and fee disclosure. Independent advisers fared better than those associated with financial institutions, but poor advisers were found in every category and sometimes even within the same firms as the better advisers.

Generally, the study found that advisers paid by commission were more likely to produce poor quality plans. Common deficiencies in plans included:

- Failing to provide an Advisory Services Guide
- Failing to show how the recommended strategy and action was appropriate for the client
- Being hard to read and 'padded' with reams of generic information
- Some planners ignoring key client requirements and not explaining why
- Recommending higher-fee investments without showing why these were better than cheaper alternatives
- Recommending a switch without showing how new investments would be better than existing investments.

What's the best way to find a financial planner?

If you can't find a planner by word of mouth, contact the Financial Planning Association (phone 1800 626 393), who will refer you to a number of licensed planners. If you're not comfortable with the first planner you see, keep on trying. Keep in mind that most planners will charge to draw up an initial plan for you, and although it can be useful to compare plans, the cost will mount up. If a planner offers you a free plan, though, watch out; it might be a standard 'off the shelf' plan, not tailored to your particular situation. In the end, it really comes down to finding a licensed planner with whom you are comfortable and who makes an effort to find out what you really need, rather than giving you a pre-packaged solution.

When should I first consult a financial planner?

You don't have to wait until you have a large sum to invest. As long as you can put aside some money every month (i.e. your Money Picture is Green), you can start off with a regular investment plan.

Tip

Financial planners aren't the same as credit counsellors; they can't really help you if you are struggling to make ends meet. As soon as you have some surplus cash, that's the time to see a planner.

What should I do before I see a planner for the first time?

Make a statement of your assets and liabilities (this is set out in Chapter 7), and put together all your important financial documents; for example, bank statements, super statements, etc. Make sure your Money Picture is up to date. The aim of all this is to help the planner embark on a fact-finding mission, to get an accurate picture of your overall finances.

Think about your life goals, and what you want to achieve from your investments. Also, think about your risk tolerance – if you want higher returns from your investments, you'll have to accept a higher risk of losing some of your money. If this would make you lose sleep at night, make sure the planner knows that you would rather take a lower return, with more security. An adviser can give you options within those parameters, but he or she can't make those important decisions for you.

The booklet 'Don't kiss your money goodbye' by the Financial Planning Association of Australia and the Australian Securities and Investment Commission gives the following checklist for choosing a financial planner:

1. Learn some investing basics (see Chapter 6).
2. Write down what you want (see Chapters 2 and 3 on setting your goals and putting together your Money Picture).
3. Deal only with licensed people (phone the ASIC information line on 1300 300 630 or go to the ASIC website at www.asic.gov.au). Are they a member of the Financial Planning Association (phone 1800 626 393)?
4. Phone the adviser beforehand and ask for a copy of their Financial Services Guide. Don't deal with them if they don't have one. It should outline the adviser's remuneration (fees, commissions, etc.) and whether the adviser works for or has links with a financial institution (for example they may be the agent of a bank or insurance company and hence may have an obligation to promote their products), what products they offer, and how they deal with customer complaints.
5. Ask what sort of research services the adviser uses (financial planners usually use research by professional research companies such as ASSIRT, who assess products, performances, fees, etc).
6. Ask for details of all fees and charges. Weigh up the costs (what are the total costs you will be paying for – commissions, fees and any other costs).
7. If the adviser tries to sign you up as a client on the spot this can be a bad sign.
8. Only deal with an adviser who has professional indemnity insurance.

Finding a lawyer

What can a lawyer do for me?

There are many different types of lawyers, and different circumstances where people need legal advice or representation. Most of us first come into contact with a lawyer when we buy our first house or unit. Other common reasons for seeing a lawyer are being injured in an accident, separating or getting a divorce, needing advice regarding an employment situation, and wanting to make a will. Anyone who is running a business will also need legal advice on leasing an office, shop or factory, employing people, preparing terms of sale for their customers, and generally complying with their legal obligations.

Choosing a lawyer

The most important thing to bear in mind when choosing a lawyer is to make sure he or she is experienced in dealing with your type of problem. This sounds obvious, but often people don't realise how specialised the legal profession is. For this reason, word of mouth can be unreliable. The fact that your friend's lawyer handled her divorce brilliantly is no guarantee that they'll do a good job with your personal injury claim.

Different types of lawyers

If you live in New South Wales, Queensland or the Northern Territory, the legal profession is divided into solicitors and barristers. This division roughly mirrors general practitioners and specialists in the medical profession; you'd normally make your first contact with a solicitor.

In Victoria, Tasmania, South Australia, Western Australia and the Australian Capital Territory, the legal profession is 'fused', i.e. a lawyer can be a barrister or a solicitor or both. Again, your first port of call will most likely be with a solicitor.

In some states (NSW, Queensland, Victoria and WA) the local law society has set up a scheme of specialist accreditation. Under this type of scheme, a lawyer must do a special course and pass an exam to be able to call him or herself an 'accredited specialist'. This is a good way for you to check that the lawyer does indeed specialise in the relevant area of law. However, the process of becoming accredited is expensive and time-consuming, so not all good lawyers will bother with it.

What's the best way to find a lawyer?

If you have a good word of mouth recommendation, and the lawyer is experienced in the relevant area of law, that's a good starting point.

However, if you don't have a word of mouth recommendation, you can ask your state law society to give you the names of a few lawyers in your local area who claim to specialise in the field of law specified. Bear in mind that lawyers nominate themselves for these lists, and the law society doesn't carry out any checks, so a law society referral is not the same as a recommendation.

The contact details for the state law societies are:

- Law Society of New South Wales
  phone (02) 9926 0333; www.lawsociety.com.au
- Law Institute of Victoria
  phone (03) 9607 9311; www.liv. asn.au
- Queensland Law Society
  phone (07) 3842 5888; www.qls. com.au
- Law Society of South Australia
  phone (08) 8229 0222; www. lssa.asn.au
- Law Society of WA
  phone (08) 9322 7877; www.lawsocietywa.asn.au
- Law Society of Tasmania
  phone (03) 6234 4133; www.taslawsociety.asn.au
- Law Society of Australian Capital Territory
  phone (02) 6247 5700; www.lawsocact.asn.au
- Law Society of Northern Territory
  phone (08) 8981 5104; www. lawsocnt.asn.au

Depending on the type of legal problem you have, some lawyers may not charge for an initial interview. The first meeting is your opportunity to ask the lawyer some relevant questions, such as:

- How long have you been working in this area of law?
- What are your fees?
- How long is my matter likely to take?
- What are my chances of success (if it's a court case)?
- Will you be doing all the work, or will some things be delegated to another lawyer in the firm, or a secretary or paralegal?
- Do you require any payment in advance for expenses?
- Do you prefer to communicate with me by fax, telephone or email?
- How often will you give me progress reports?

The answers to these questions, and the general rapport you establish with the lawyer, should give you a feeling as to whether or not you will have confidence in their ability to represent you.

Is there any way I can save on fees?

For some types of transaction, typically property work, lawyers will charge a flat fee. This makes it easy to compare costs between firms.

For work that is more open-ended, including virtually all court cases, lawyers charge by the hour (also known as 'time costing'). The lawyer will charge you for all time spent on your file; even a quick telephone conversation will be added to your bill.

Some tips for minimising legal fees

- Get a written fee estimate before the lawyer starts doing any work for you.
- The initial fee estimate (also sometimes called a 'costs agreement') should include an undertaking to inform you in writing as soon as the lawyer becomes aware that the total costs will be higher than expected.
- If you are being charged on a 'time costing basis', try not to waste the lawyer's time. You can avoid wasting time by providing all documents requested by the lawyer quickly, and not making unnecessary or overly long telephone calls to them.

- If you are involved in a court case, try to settle it as soon as possible. Don't hold out for a result that your lawyer tells you is unrealistic.
- If you are comparing flat fee quotes, make sure that you have a full description of all the work included (for example, will the lawyer charge extra for incidental tasks, such as helping with finance?).
- Lawyers' bills also have a component called 'disbursements'. This means expenses that the lawyer has paid out on your behalf, such as the cost of title searches, or court filing fees. Sometimes lawyers make a profit on disbursements, for example rounding up expenses such as photocopying or courier charges. It should be clear from the outset how much the likely disbursements in your case will be, and on what basis are they charged. When comparing fees, check also that the disbursements are comparable. For example, some lawyers will charge the cost of an agent attending a property settlement as a disbursement; others may include it in the flat fee.

Lawyers will often ask you to pay money in advance, before they do any work for you. Sometimes this is to pay for anticipated disbursements, and sometimes it is to protect the lawyer if you don't pay your bill. Particularly if you are a new client, you may find that the lawyer will not want to do too much work for you unless they are covered by an advance payment. If you pay money in advance, the lawyer must bank it in a trust account and cannot withdraw any of it to pay for fees until he or she has sent you a bill first. However, withdrawals can be made from time to time to pay for disbursements that have previously been disclosed to you.

How NOT to do it

Don't be the client from hell! Here are seven guaranteed ways to damage the relationship with your accountant, financial planner or lawyer:

1. Leave important documents behind when you turn up for a meeting.

2. When telling your story, ramble all over the place; take your time to get to the point (or maybe never get there at all).
3. Ask (or worse, insist) that your adviser does something unethical or illegal.
4. Pay your account only after months of reminder calls, and/or haggle fiercely.
5. Deny, hide or gloss over inconvenient truths.
6. Change your mind a lot.
7. Don't accept the advice you are given. Shop around for an adviser who will tell you what you want to hear.

To get the best result from your adviser, don't treat him or her as simply a 'hired gun'. You'll stand out from the other clients and cement what should be a mutually enriching relationship if you can always give positive feedback where it's due. As a final tip, to guarantee the eternal appreciation of your adviser, recommend him or her to all your friends. A good recommendation will benefit everyone.

CHAPTER 9

Your relationship

Your relationship can have a very significant effect on your finances, and vice versa. A good relationship can bring huge financial benefits, and not having to worry about money will eliminate a common source of friction between partners.

Living together certainly cuts down on your combined cost of living; housing costs are less, and lots of other expenses can be shared – transport, insurance, electricity, food, etc. Having a partner to rely on can give you more flexibility in life – time off work to study, or have children, or start a business. With high housing prices in some parts of Australia it's extremely difficult, if not impossible, to borrow enough money to buy a home on only one income. Together you and your partner can achieve a lot more than either of you could have alone.

Managing joint finances

There are different ways a couple might decide to manage their finances.

On one hand, there's the 'I'm in control' model, where one partner has complete control over all finances. This model puts the non-controlling partner in a vulnerable situation. If the controlling partner is a competent financial manager and the relationship is strong, then it can work. If either of those assumptions fails, the person who has given up control may be vulnerable.

At the other end of the spectrum is the 'strictly separate' model, with both partners having their own separate bank accounts and sharing joint expenses in an agreed proportion. If both partners are working and earning reasonably similar salaries, this can be a very workable arrangement. If circumstances change, for example if one partner stops work for a while and is financially dependent on the other, the 'strictly separate' regime may have to be modified.

Most couples fall somewhere in between, with a joint bank account to pay for joint expenses, and individual accounts for whatever is left over.

Discussing finances with your partner can be very tricky. It raises a whole host of sensitive issues, such as whether the person who earns more money has more say in financial matters, how much each partner should be keeping as 'private' money, and generally how much trust there is in the relationship. If either partner has children from a previous relationship, the cost of supporting those children can be a source of friction in the new relationship. If one partner is very conservative with money, and the other a spendthrift, how are you going to reconcile these different approaches?

As with all relationship issues, it's important to be honest about your finances, and to do your best to understand the other person's point of view. Our attitudes to money are formed very early in our childhood (as we saw in Chapter 1), and they are not always easy to change. It can be hard to watch your partner make what you think are disastrous financial decisions, or to live with someone whose attitude towards money is opposed to your own. Try to come up with some common financial objectives, for which you can allocate a portion of your joint funds without argument, but at the same time, keep some of your finances separate. Think about couples you know who manage their finances successfully; they have probably agreed on their main financial objectives, and work as a team to support each other financially and in other ways.

Barrier buster

Have you and your partner ever sat down together and openly discussed your financial goals? It's worth doing, especially if you focus on positive goals you can achieve.

Julie and Steve are in their forties and have two children. Julie is in charge of their joint finances.

When we first started living together, fifteen years ago, we kept our finances fairly separate. We paid for everything separately out of our own accounts. As time went on, we opened a joint bank account for joint expenses. Gradually over time our finances became more and more entwined, and we used the joint account more and more. When I stopped work to have our first child, we reorganised our banking and closed our individual accounts, just using the joint account for everything. Now that I am back working and we have some money to invest, we have reorganised our banking again so that we have a joint account for all our everyday expenses, and individual accounts to pay for our separate investments.

I am the one in charge of our finances; I pay all the bills and keep track of our mortgage. Both of us have access to all the money in our accounts, but I'm the only one who uses it. Steve doesn't have time to do this, and he's not really interested. He trusts me. Our system works because we have similar attitudes towards money and we agree on our major financial goals.

No matter what arrangement you come to, it's important to know exactly what is going on in your joint finances, and to have some financial independence within the relationship. If you are really bogged down and can't agree on anything with your partner, get some professional help from a counsellor. Financial incompatibility is too important to ignore.

Does your relationship inhibit or support your earning capacity?

Sometimes, your relationship can hold you back in your efforts to achieve financial fitness. It can be hard to control your career and your money if you don't have your partner's enthusiastic support.

Annette faced the obstacle of a partner who wanted to control her through limiting her financial independence.

When my youngest child started school, it was time for me to embark on the career I had always wanted. Before I could start work, I had to do a course to get the qualifications I needed. My husband didn't actively discourage me, but I do remember that the course fee could be paid up-front, or spread over two instalments. My husband's attitude was, 'Well, let's just pay the first instalment for now.' I didn't interpret this as an encouraging sign.

When I finished the course and started work, I never felt that the money I earned was my own. My husband would say, 'You've got too much money piling up in your account' and he'd just clear the money out from time to time, so I could never amass a serious amount.

Although he didn't try to stop me from working, he did make sure that I wouldn't have any financial independence. For example (this was in the days before compulsory superannuation), I had the option of joining a very generous superannuation scheme. My husband strongly objected to me joining the scheme, claiming that it would conflict with his own plans. Later, when our marriage broke up and I went to join the superannuation scheme, I had to make up a lot of retrospective payments which really set me back for a while.

Now that I've retired, I'm so glad I joined that scheme. It was a real life saver and is now my main source of income.

Another way that a relationship can affect your career is if your partner works for a company where the promotion path is dependent on frequent relocation. Unless you've got an easily portable profession, it can be a real problem. Both partners have some hard choices; one can try to move into a career more compatible with the constant moves, the other can try to change their company's policy or look for another job. If neither of these options is possible, you're facing a choice between career and relationship. Some couples compromise by taking it in turns to follow their career.

What can you do if there's some aspect of your relationship that is holding you back? Sometimes it's not really about money at all; financial problems can be a reflection of more basic issues of power and control in the relationship, as would seem to be the case in Annette's story. Annette did a number of things that improved her situation; she invested in herself by getting the qualifications necessary for the job she wanted, she kept on working, and she made up as much of her superannuation payments as she could. She is now financially independent.

Pre-nuptial or cohabitation agreements

Most of us go into a marriage or de facto relationship thinking and hoping that it will last; and, believe it or not, most relationships (or at least most marriages – there are no statistics for de factos) do last the distance. Even though the divorce rate is high, it is still less than 50%. When you are happy in your relationship, it seems harsh and unromantic to think about what can go wrong with your finances if you split up.

If you are contemplating a relationship, or even if you're already in one, have a think about whether a pre-nuptial or cohabitation agreement would be a good idea for you and your partner. This type of agreement is not right for everyone, but even if you decide not to go ahead with it, going through the exercise of honestly talking about your finances and expectations will be very helpful.

'Pre-nuptial' means 'before marriage', and a pre-nuptial agreement is an agreement couples sign before they are married to say who gets what in the event of divorce. If you're not married, but living together, you can sign a similar agreement, called a 'cohabitation agreement'.

Who should have a pre-nuptial or cohabitation agreement?

Until recently, married couples could not enter into binding pre-nuptial agreements. Under the Family Law Act, pre-nuptial agreements were not enforceable. However, the Family Law Act was amended in 2000 and now allows for married couples to sign legally binding agreements, either before or during their marriage. De facto couples can enter into binding cohabitation agreements under state legislation.

Lawyers sometimes disagree on whether pre-nuptial or cohabitation agreements are a good thing. Often it will depend on your individual circumstances. The pitfalls include:

- Just mentioning the topic might finish the relationship! This really can happen, so you have to tread very carefully in bringing up the subject. Maybe those relationships that ended were bound to fail anyway, and the argument over the agreement just hastened the end. Arguing over money is a common cause of problems in a relationship, and if you can't agree on what will go into your agreement at the beginning when things are good, it's not a very encouraging sign.
- If the relationship is unequal, it can be hard to make sure that the financially weaker partner is entering into the agreement freely and voluntarily. Agreements are only enforceable if both partners get a lawyer to sign a certificate saying that they've obtained legal advice and that the agreement is fair and reasonable. This will be easier to do if everything is split 50/50, reflecting equal contributions; harder if one party will get much more than the other.
- Circumstances can change. Ten or twenty years after the agreement is signed, all sorts of unexpected things can happen – for example, babies, retrenchment, illness or inheritance. For this reason, agreements are not usually recommended for young couples.

Couples who would most benefit from an agreement are older and reasonably equal in their assets and earning capacity. The benefits for them are:

- The agreement sets out exactly what assets they bring to the relationship – usually, in the event of a break-up, each partner will retain his or her own assets.
- Entering into an agreement should alleviate the fears of family or adult children that their prospective inheritance is at risk if a parent has started a new relationship.

Michelle and Alex are a good example of a couple whose circumstances are right for a de facto agreement. They are in their forties and have both been married before; now they each have their own assets and income.

Before Alex and I started living together, we had a de facto agreement drawn up. Although I have more assets than Alex, he was the one who raised it. He said to me, 'If we move in together I want to make sure we do this properly. You have more assets than me and I want to make sure you're protected. I want everything set down in writing.'

It was very easy and straightforward; there was no negotiation, we agreed on everything. Our agreement is a very simple document. If we break up, we each get to keep the assets we started with, and anything we acquire afterwards will be split according to who paid for it. The agreement will be automatically terminated if we have a child together or if we marry, in which case we will have a fresh agreement prepared.

I think having an agreement done is sensible. It didn't have any effect on our relationship, but our relationship was very good to begin with. Maybe it would be different if one of us was being supported by the other; I can see that might be tricky, but it was easy for us because we are equally capable of supporting ourselves.

Putting an agreement together

If you and your partner have decided that an agreement would be appropriate for your circumstances, you'll have to decide what goes in it. The first step is to make three lists of assets: those you each own individually, and those you own jointly. Usually people will want to keep the assets they already own, but of course you have to decide if this is right for you.

The next step is to think about who will own assets acquired in the future. Will everything be jointly owned, or will the assets be owned by the person who paid for them? This is a reflection of how intertwined your finances are. The first alternative has the virtue of simplicity, but might not necessarily be fair to both of you. If you go for the second alternative, it might get messy later, trying to work out who paid for what.

A third alternative is to say that everything will be jointly owned, except where an asset is explicitly acquired in the name of one party using their own money.

There will be other issues to consider in the agreement:

• Do you want the agreement to override your rights to take each other to court if you separate? (Usually this is the whole point of having an agreement, but the agreement has to explicitly spell it out.)
• Do you want to use the agreement to stop each other from challenging your wills if one of you dies?
• What if your circumstances change unexpectedly – for example, you get an inheritance, or have children?

Especially if you are at the dewy-eyed early stages of your relationship, the notion of sitting down to talk about separating and splitting your assets will sound unromantic and cynical. No-one likes thinking about things going wrong, let alone actively planning for it. Think of it this way; if the relationship is happy and successful, the agreement will stay in the bottom drawer and there's no harm done. If things do go sour, by having had a plan drawn up when you were co-operating and agreeing with each other, you will have protected yourself against the stress and expense of a lengthy settlement negotiation.

Divorce or separation

What if the worst happens and your relationship breaks down? You will need some basic knowledge of how the legal system works to resolve the financial issues between yourself and your ex-partner.

When a marriage or de facto relationship breaks down, the immediate financial impact is almost always negative for both people involved. The most obvious cost is having to pay for two houses or flats instead of one, and most other living expenses will also be higher. There's not much you can do about that. What you can control is how quickly and fairly you and your ex-partner *can* come to an agreement, to minimise legal costs and protect yourself from an unfair settlement.

It helps to have a basic understanding of the way in which the law deals with the splitting of joint assets.

Family law is split into state and federal laws. If you're married, you will come under the Family Law Act, which is federal legislation. Therefore, the law covers all states. If you are not married, you may come under the definition of 'de facto relationship' under the de facto laws that apply in your state.

Owning assets before and after separation

During a marriage or de facto relationship, your property and debts are either held individually or jointly with your partner. Sometimes it's obvious who has what; for example, an asset such as a house or car will be registered in one or both names. Other types of assets are not so clear, for example furniture or computer equipment. At law, whoever paid for the asset is considered the owner. This isn't always easy to establish.

If there were no Family Law Act or de facto legislation, property would be owned by whoever had paid for it, regardless of any other circumstances. The only way to change ownership would be to argue that the person who owned the property intended to own it on trust for the other party to the relationship, which is very difficult to establish.

Therefore, the aim of the legislation is to give a court power to change the ownership of property, taking into account the full circumstances of the relationship. The court isn't restricted to the narrow issues of who paid for what; the court looks at the circumstances of the entire relationship. This will include direct and indirect contributions from each partner, both financial and non-financial. The court will also consider who has responsibility for the children, the parties' respective earning capacities and other financial resources, and any other financial needs they have. (However, note our comments further on regarding the different approaches taken under the Family Law Act and the de facto laws.)

There's no set formula for dividing property after separation, because everyone's circumstances are so different.

How long after separation can I get a divorce?

Under the Family Law Act, either partner can get a divorce after 12 months' separation. If you get back together again for more than three months, and then separate again, the 12 months starts running again. If the time you get back together is less than three months, you can add together the periods of separation before and after.

What share of the assets will I get?

Generally speaking, this will depend on past contributions and future income and needs. If one partner has made a much greater contribution to the assets of the marriage than the other, or has greater future needs (for example, having to care for children), then that partner's share will be increased.

Does it make any difference if you're married or living together?

The wording of the Family Law Act and the de facto legislation is different, and the legislation is interpreted by different courts; respectively, the Family Court and the state Supreme Courts. Generally, the Family Court will give more weight than the Supreme Courts to non-financial contributions. Therefore, a partner whose major contribution has been non-financial, i.e. home-making or raising children, will get a bigger share of the assets if married than if in a de facto relationship. A partner whose major contribution has been financial, i.e. they have directly paid for the assets, will get a bigger share if covered by the de facto legislation.

Another area of difference between the two court systems is that if you were in a de facto relationship, the Supreme Court is more likely to make a costs order in favour of the successful party, whereas costs orders are rarely made in the Family Court. Whether this helps you or not will depend on whether you win the case (in which you can get some of your legal costs paid by your ex-partner) or lose, in which case you may be ordered to pay your ex-partner's legal costs as well as your own.

Finally, the Family Court now has the power to order super-annuation funds to split up a person's superannuation entitlement, so that it can be divided between the husband and wife. This does not apply to people in a de facto relationship.

Do I need a lawyer?

You don't need a lawyer to get divorced. The Family Court Registry in every capital city has a divorce kit which has all the necessary forms and sets out all the steps you need to take to apply for a divorce without a lawyer. If you are in a de facto relationship, there's no equivalent procedure to a divorce. Unlike divorce, for de facto couples there's no official piece of paper to confirm that the relationship has ended.

To work out a property settlement, you'll almost certainly need to see a lawyer. If you enter into a property settlement agreement, under either the Family Law Act or de facto legislation, it won't be binding unless all assets have been disclosed, and both partners have received independent legal advice. Because there's no set formula for dividing property, it can be hard to know if a settlement is fair or not. A lawyer who specialises in family law will be able to guide you as to what you should realistically expect to achieve.

What's the difference between a 'property settlement' and 'proceedings'?

These two terms are sometimes used interchangeably, to describe the entire process of finalising marital property. A property settlement is an agreement reached by the parties. 'Proceedings' means a court case, where the decision is made by a judge. It's very common for parties to start court proceedings, by filing an application for property orders, partly to get the ball rolling on negotiations, and partly to make sure they don't miss the deadline (in the Family Court, 12 months after divorce). Once proceedings are started, the court encourages the parties to come to their own settlement agreement, to avoid a full hearing before a judge.

Traps to avoid

For most people, going through a separation is a difficult and upsetting time; hardly the best circumstances in which to be making major decisions about your financial future. It's at this time, soon after breaking up, that people are under the most pressure to get their affairs sorted out. One or sometimes both partners will need to find somewhere new to live, joint debts have to be sorted out quickly, assets divided up while they can still be found. It's a very tense time all round, and coming to a final settlement is normally a huge relief.

These are the main traps to look out for that will increase the financial pain of settling your finances with your ex partner:

1. IF YOU AND YOUR EX-PARTNER CAN'T AGREE ON A PROPERTY SETTLEMENT QUICKLY. The longer it takes for you and your ex-partner to agree on a settlement, the higher will be the legal costs for both of you. Over 90% of separating couples reach agreement on their property settlement out of court. Hardly anyone goes right through to finish their court case, because it's very expensive and there's no guarantee that you'll get a better result. Also, if one party is unscrupulous, any delay in settling will give them more time to hide or downgrade the value of their assets.

Tom and his ex-wife eventually settled their case after the court hearing had started; his story shows how much the delay in settling cost both of them.

We finally settled our property case about two years after our first attempt at settlement via mediation. The settlement we reached was much the same as what I had originally proposed at the mediation. The offer my ex-wife made at the mediation was completely unacceptable to me; I knew I had nothing to lose by pressing on, even though my total legal costs came to more than $50,000. Her costs were even higher; about $75,000. Why were her costs so much higher? I think there were two reasons. Her lawyers seemed to be inefficient, some days sending my solicitors three or four letters on the same day. Also, my ex was relatively disorganised and her lawyers would have had to put in a lot more hours to gather information. I saved legal costs by being very organised, spending hours putting together the financial documents my lawyers asked for (bank statements, tax returns, credit card statements, bills, etc), and on some occasions I wrote the first draft of my affidavits (i.e. statements to be used in court).

Ultimately I felt the money I spent on my lawyers was worthwhile, in that I had to do it to get a reasonable result. On the other hand, I know that my ex-wife deeply resented the amount she had spent on her lawyers, especially as she ended up agreeing to something she could have had two years ago at the mediation. I think she had felt that if she stood her ground long enough I would cave in. Then when we were on the courtroom steps she finally realised what she was risking.

Both Tom and especially his ex-wife could have saved an enormous amount of money if they'd been able to settle their property dispute at the earlier opportunity. Luckily for Tom, he resisted pressure to succumb to another big trap.

2. AGREEING TO A BAD PROPERTY SETTLEMENT Almost everyone will come out of a settlement negotiation feeling they could or should have got a better result. Sometimes people settle for much less than they should. Common reasons are:

- Ex-partners successfully hiding assets or misrepresenting the value of their assets
- Bullying behaviour by ex-partners (you'll settle for anything just to get it over and done with)
- Needing a quick settlement to get enough money to live on or pay off debts

Standing up for yourself in a property negotiation can be scary, as Ann's story demonstrates.

It took about seven years to finalise my property settlement after my marriage broke up. During that time my husband made payments for the kids, but as the children became independent the payments were reduced and I could see that I was never going to have a proper lump sum that I could call my own. So I went to a lawyer and negotiated a final settlement.

I felt sure that I settled for less than I was entitled to — I think I ended up with about 10% of the total assets. Why did I settle for so little? I wasn't sure how strong my case was. Although my barrister said

I had a good case, I didn't have much confidence in him. Also, I knew that my husband would have the very best lawyers, and I suspected that he was hiding some of his assets. He was a hard person to take on.

I truly don't know if I would have got more money if I'd gone to court. At the time, I was just glad to get it over and done with.

Tips to help you get the most out of the process

- Make sure you know what has been going on in your relationship. Don't delegate all the household finances to your partner.
- Don't sign any financial documents, such as guarantees, for your partner unless you fully understand what your liability could be.
- Avoid a fully contested hearing before a judge. If you settle out of court, you have the advantage of certainty; you'll know what result you're getting, and it will be something you can live with. Of course, if this is impossible, e.g. if your ex-partner won't come to an acceptable agreement, then you're better off putting the decision into the court's hands.

Sexually transmitted debt

Apart from divorce (although often the two can surface together), a threat to your finances connected to your relationship is 'sexually transmitted debt'. Sexually transmitted debt is a way of describing the situation where someone 'catches' their partner's debts, usually by signing a joint loan agreement, or going guarantor. If things are going well in the relationship it might seem like a mere formality to sign the documents for the bank; you might not bother to read the documents carefully, or might not be given time to read them. If things are bad, you could be bullied or manipulated into signing.

Sometimes people are told that they must sign a guarantee, or their partner's business will go broke. Or they are misled into thinking that there is a limit to their liability, not realising that if there is a default on the loan, the amount owing to the bank can blow out to much more than the amount originally borrowed, due to penalty interest clauses, legal costs, etc.

Often the reason the bank is demanding the guarantee in the first place is that it has reason to believe that the main borrower is in financial trouble, and may not be able to pay back the loan.

Signing any of these documents could lead to sexually transmitted debt

- A bank or store credit card application form
- Shop credit of the '24-month interest-free' variety
- An application for a loan from a bank, finance company, or other financial institution
- A guarantee of another person's loan obligations
- A 'director's guarantee', if you are both directors of a company
- An application for a bank account with an overdraft facility

By signing any of the documents listed above, you are putting yourself up to be fully responsible to pay *all* of the debt to the credit provider. If for whatever reason your partner is unable to pay the debt, the credit provider is under no obligation to chase that person first. It will take the line of least resistance, which is to pursue the person with the most accessible income, or the most assets.

Sometimes sexually transmitted debt can sneak up on you, as you find yourself taking on more and more debt to pay for joint expenses. This is what happened to Yvette.

Shortly after I moved to Melbourne to start my career as a flight attendant, I met my boyfriend. He was five years younger than me and was working as an apprentice, which meant he did not earn much. Most times I would pay for our dinners and outings.

About three years into our relationship, by which time we were living together, we wanted to take a holiday together and go to the USA. Working for an airline, I was able to get a cheap flight deal. My boyfriend didn't have the money but I said I would pay for him and he promised to pay me back.

While on holidays in the USA, I ended up paying for the lot – all our expenses, shopping and clothes. I put everything on my credit cards. He did pay for half the accommodation and kept saying he would pay me back for the rest. He'd also finished his apprenticeship and had moved onto a better-paying job.

Thinking back, I should have asked for the money as soon as we got back, but as time went by, I let it go. He was still on a relatively low wage and I paid for most things. I really thought we were going to be together, even get married. My credit card bills escalated from our joint expenses – I paid for our phone bills, the mobiles, electricity, our groceries. I can now see we were living beyond our means and I was paying for it all.

My credit cards reached their limit and I was struggling to keep up the minimum payments – this was causing me a lot of stress. Five years into our relationship, he left me for someone else.

At the time he left, the lease for the unit was in my name. He left me with all the rent and bills to pay. I'm still having a hard time paying off the bills. I even applied for a loan, hoping to pay off my debts, but because my credit cards were over the limit, the bank would not give me the loan.

I blame myself, just as much as I blame him; I bought things for him and I allowed this to go on. I should have put my foot down and insisted he help with the bills.

I left the unit and now I am renting a much cheaper one. I'm trying to keep my expenses down and I want to clear my credit cards. I truly thought we were going to stay together. I was devastated when he left me. But I know now it is for the best. I just heard from his mother that he is going overseas again and guess who is paying for his ticket – yes, his new girlfriend. He is doing it again.

So what's the solution to sexually transmitted debt?

- If your partner is not making an equal contribution to your joint expenses, don't let it get to the stage where the amount of your combined debts will seriously jeopardise your finances, as Yvette did.
- Understand your partner's financial situation. It's all very well to keep some things private in a relationship, but unless you've agreed to keep all your finances strictly separate (which means no joint debts at all), money should never be a 'no-go' area.
- *Never* sign a document you don't understand. Once you turn 18, the law is that unless there are extraordinary circumstances, you're deemed to understand and agree to any document you sign.
- Get good independent professional advice (not from your partner's or the bank's adviser). A lawyer can help you understand the full ramifications of what you're signing. If you're asked to support a partner's business, an accountant can advise you if the business is financially viable.
- Even if you have a pre-nuptial or de facto agreement with your partner, it won't help you if the bank comes knocking on your door. The problem of sexually transmitted debt is that you've created your own direct relationship with the credit provider – the terms of any agreement you may have come to with your partner are irrelevant, as far as the credit provider is concerned.
- If it's too late, and you're being chased for your partner's debts, you need to look at your options realistically. A credit counsellor can help schedule repayments. A lawyer can help you decide if it's worth taking on the bank (occasionally the consumer does win!) or pursuing your partner. The very worst thing you can do is nothing, because the problem won't go away.

Hopefully, having read this chapter, you're not packing your bags to head off to a monastery or nunnery just yet. Relationships and parenthood sometimes look like hard work (and often are!), but for most of us the rewards are worth it. Undoubtedly there are risks as well as benefits, including big financial risks. But the best things in life, including relationships, involve some level of risk. Go in with your eyes open and don't be afraid to look after your own interests; that way you'll be protected if things go bad.

CHAPTER 10

Your family

Our society has come a long way from the days when children were sent to work in mines and factories to help support their families. These days, we support our children, often well into their twenties, with no real expectation that the favour will ever be returned. We four authors are very familiar with the financial issues that come with parenthood, as we all have children.

The rewards we get from our kids are enormous, but they are obviously non-financial (unless of course any of our offspring becomes a professional golfer or tennis player!). Having said that, it's not a bad idea to embark on parenthood with a realistic idea of what you're in for.

It can be very scary exercise to add up the real costs of having children. It goes way beyond the obvious things, such as food, nappies and, later on, school fees. There are less obvious expenses – a bigger house, a bigger car, only being able to go away during school holidays when everything is more expensive. As children grow into teenagers, they become more expensive for their parents. They eat more, they cost more to take away on holidays, they start to go out with their friends and clamour for expensive designer clothes and mobile phones and so the list goes on.

A major cost of having children is the lost income as one or both parents take time out of the workforce. Research by the ANU

Centre for Economic Policy Research found that a woman with average education who has one child will incur a lifetime earnings loss of about $336,000. Recent research by the National Centre of Social and Economic Modelling found that the cost of raising a child from birth to age 20 is $264,000 for the first child and an extra $184,000 for the second child; that's nearly half a million dollars in direct expenses, not counting the loss of income!

Population trends

If the cost puts you off having any, or more, children, you're not alone. The natural birthrate in Australia is declining, and therefore the Australian population is getting older.

This population trend is a direct result of fewer couples having children, and those who do having smaller families. Australians are also delaying having children, with the median age of first-time mothers increasing in the last decade from 26 to 29 years old. Waiting longer to have children usually gives women more time to establish their careers, and allows couples to be in a better financial situation generally. It's also a reflection of modern life, where people on average take longer to finish their education, travel and establish a career, compared to their parents.

Even though we try our best to fit babies into our careers and busy lives, the best-laid plans can go astray, as Jane's story shows.

When I became pregnant with my first child, I was working for a very large company. I planned to take nine months' maternity leave, and gave the company plenty of notice.

The day before I was due to return to work, I was made redundant. Instead of finding a temporary worker to take my place while I was on leave, the company had put on a full-time permanent replacement. I had been concerned about this at the time, but the company had assured me that my job was safe, and that my department was expanding permanently.

The immediate impact was not too bad, in that I received a good payout and an offer to go back part-time as a contractor for a few months. However, during those few months, I found it very difficult to get another job. In interviews, when I told the story of how I had left my old job, I was often asked if I was planning to have more children. There was no way for me to answer this question honestly without completely destroying my chances. (Authors' note: all these companies have acted illegally!)

In the end, I decided to start my own business. The first few years were very tough, and definitely forced us to postpone having a second child longer than we had planned. Maybe I could have taken my old company to court, but I was worried that this would hamper my ability to find another job even more.

Instead of the minor career blip I had expected, my first pregnancy resulted in a major career change. From talking to my friends who have had babies, my situation was not that unusual. It seems to be fairly rare to just pick up the pieces of your career where you'd left off before having children. In the end, starting my business turned out to be a blessing in disguise; it allowed me to spend a lot more time with my children than I otherwise would have, and led to some wonderful opportunities.

Workplace issues

Jane's experience is all too common. Although in Australia it is illegal for an employer to sack an employee due to pregnancy, and in fact companies must keep workers' jobs open while they take maternity leave, there are often practical and financial difficulties in taking an employer to court. A report of the Human Rights and Equal Opportunity Commission (HREOC) in 1999 found that 'one of the greatest disincentives to lodge a formal external complaint is the widespread perception that complainants are troublemakers. Making an external complaint is often perceived by employees as likely to hinder future job prospects.'

Problems in the workforce are not confined to women. The HREOC report also found that despite a federal government law providing for one week's unpaid paternity leave for a male employee to attend the birth of a child (some awards, enterprise agreements or individual contracts may have additional leave entitlements for fathers), many workplaces have cultures that discourage men from taking such leave.

The concept of the family-friendly workplace is a very topical one at the moment. Some high profile men are downsizing their jobs (and their pay packets) to spend more time with their children.

This can be a difficult option, though, as David's story shows.

I would really like to change the way I work. I've got two small children, and I see very little of them during the week. I work for a firm where it's expected of all the professional staff to put in enormous hours, at least 10 hours on weekdays and often to come in on weekends as well. I earn good money, which we really need because our lifestyle is very expensive and will only get worse as the kids get older. It's a real catch-22; I need this sort of job to provide for my kids, but the job is stopping me from being the sort of father I'd like to be.

I'm due for a pay rise later this year, which we're prepared to do without. I'm thinking of asking if I can trade in the pay rise for fewer hours. In theory this shouldn't cost the firm anything, but I'm afraid it will upset the office culture.

Although it is rare for a man's career to be interrupted by having children in the same way that it often is for a woman's, men aren't completely unaffected. Most are very aware of the additional financial responsibility that comes with having children, especially if they are the sole income earner. Men can feel that their career options are limited once they have children, in the sense that the pressure is on for them to go for, or keep, high-paying jobs.

Timing

Timing is important too. If your children are born at a time when you'd otherwise be studying or starting out in the workforce, it can take years to get back on track, as Debbie's story shows.

When I was 20 I fell pregnant. It was planned, even though we didn't have much money and I had to go back to work full-time when the baby was three months old.

A few years later my marriage broke up. I met my second husband, and had two more children while I was in my twenties. We moved to live in Brisbane, and for years I only picked up a few temporary jobs.

It was always in the back of my mind that my options were still open because I had done the HSC; I could always go back and do some more study. Finally I think turning 40 was the trigger I needed to take some action. My youngest daughter was in high school and fairly independent. I was getting miserable and depressed staying at home with no money and nothing to do.

I've enrolled in a primary school teaching course and I've finished the first year. I'm pretty much guaranteed a job at the end of it; in particular, there's a shortage of teachers in the bush, which I'd love to do (and my husband is more than happy to follow me). I looked at other courses. For a while I was interested in doing law, but I spoke to the Law Society about my chances of getting a job. They told me it would be tough, that most employers want to hire young lawyers out of uni, and I'd probably have to do volunteer work to get experience. That didn't appeal to me; I really need to earn some money.

I'll teach for as long as I can, but I might only have 15 years by the time I finish the course. I love my daughters and I don't regret having had them when I was so young, but I hope that their options will be wider than mine were.

Minimising the financial impact of having children

Practise living on one salary

Living on one salary for, say, six months before the baby is born has two benefits: firstly, it should give a real boost to your savings, and secondly, it won't be such a financial shock when the baby comes.

Find out if you're entitled to any help from the government

Check with the Family Assistance Office, part of Centrelink. The number to call is 13 61 50.

Look at your commitments

Starting a family is a good time to really look at your major commitments: rent, mortgage, personal loan or credit card repayments.

If you have high-interest loans as well as a mortgage, it's almost certainly worthwhile consolidating all your debt at home loan rates. If you're worried about interest rates going up, you could fix part or all of your home loan. You can speak to your lender about reducing your monthly repayments to just cover the interest on your loan temporarily, until your finances improve. If you don't have a mortgage but do have multiple credit cards, see if you can consolidate the debt onto the card with the lowest interest rate.

Accept all offers

Chances are, once you spread the word that there's a baby on the way, you'll get some very kind offers of hand-me-down clothes, furniture, prams, etc. Remember, if someone has offered you their baby paraphernalia, you'll be doing them a big favour to take it off their hands and out of their house. We have all done this ourselves and still do today.

If you're lucky enough to have grandparents close by who are happy to babysit, that's another way to save considerable amounts of money.

Look at ways to make money

The original party plan product was Tupperware; now there's a mind-boggling array of products sold at parties, from kids' toys to sex toys. Party plan selling is often targeted towards parents who are out of the mainstream workforce.

Adele started when her kids were aged one and two and a half, and worked her way through the ranks during the next six years.

In the six years I did party plan, I worked with three different schemes, selling children's clothing, fashion jewellery and women's clothing. I started out as a sales consultant, and then became a manager, with a few sales consultants reporting to me. The real money is in recruiting as many sales consultants as you can to work underneath you, because you get a proportion of all their commissions.

I got to the point where I was doing quite well financially – on average I would make from $3000 to $6000 a month. It's an easy job *to do with kids, because the parties are usually at night, or if there's one on during the day you can take the kids with you. You do need a supportive partner to look after the kids at night.*

Anyone can do party plan – there are no formal qualifications. You need to have a certain amount of drive and determination, and good people skills. It's enjoyable work, and you meet a lot of new people.

After a while I started to feel burnt out; as I got more successful, it became more demanding, with people ringing at all hours. After six years I'd had enough and gave it away, but it was a good way for me to make money while my children were little.

If you're looking at signing on with a party plan company, make sure it's legitimate. Some plans make money by getting their consultants on the lowest rung of the ladder to pay substantial amounts to buy stock in advance that they then find difficult to offload. Be careful about paying too much up-front, and talk to a few existing consultants before you commit yourself.

Networking can be another good way of making extra money. Jobs often come up through word of mouth.

Kelly picked up some teaching work this way.

When my baby was just four months old, I got some teaching work through a friend of a friend, who had a commitment and needed someone to fill in for him one night a week for a few months. It was easy to do, I could prepare at home while the baby was asleep, and it made a nice break to get out one night a week.

Make the most of things that are free (or almost free)
- Parks and beaches
- Shopping centre entertainment
- Early childhood centres
- Libraries – not just for books, but CDs, videos and toys too
- Playgroup – to find one, ask at your local early childhood centre
- Start or join a babysitting club with friends

Set some money aside

When your baby is born, and you're wondering how you'll cope during the expensive years to come, i.e. high school and college/university, the best thing you've got going for you is time. Twelve to eighteen years is a good long time for an investment to mature.

There are some specialist education funds which mature when your child reaches high school or university age. These can have tax advantages, but are inflexible; you may not be able to get your money back if your child doesn't go on to higher education.

You should also look into managed funds, either to invest a lump sum (this may be a better gift from grandparents than a fancy pram) and forget about it, or to contribute small amounts over time. Any income earned should be reinvested, to maximise the effect of compound interest, so that the investment will be returning interest on a higher sum every year.

Blended families and single parents

The financial pressures of having children are magnified in non-traditional families. Blended families have to cope with one or both partners bearing the costs of raising children from a previous relationship; single families suffer the obvious disadvantage of surviving on only one income. Falling in love with someone who already has children, or becoming a single parent, are often not what people really plan for. By the time it's happened, you're right in the middle of it and it's too late for any advance preparation.

When finances are tight, the first thing to do is go back to your Money Picture (from Chapter 3). Accept that your picture might be Amber for a few years; as long as you are not getting further and further into debt, it's okay to tread water for this expensive time of your life. Go through all the money-saving tips in this book; think about your goals and priorities. See what help you can get from your extended family and friends in the form of helping out with the children, career networking, general friendship and support.

The future – teaching your children about money

There are no classes at school and virtually no courses or programs that help us train and educate our children about money. So how do we ensure they have the information, the knowledge and experience they need to manage their money in a highly competitive and dramatically changing world? This is a challenge for any parent.

Our children are growing up in a world where ATM machines produce money as if by magic. Payments are made on websites or on the telephone – it's a world where no-one has a 'savings book', only direct transfers, access cards and credit cards. In this 'virtual' world of money exchange it can be more difficult to see and grasp the concept of where the money is coming from, how it can be saved and how we decide when we can afford to spend it. We are a long way from the piggy banks and jam jars that some of us grew up with. It is easy to see how children may grow up not understanding the basics of saving and managing their cashflow and their money. The scary thing is that most will get credit cards before they have practised the basics of earning and managing their money.

The world our children will live in will be very different to the one we grew up in. It is already getting easier to fall into debt. Aggressive marketing campaigns such as 'free mobile phones', easily obtainable credit cards, the push for designer gear and name brands – as well as credit facilities for just about everything – have already led to a massive increase in debt. It is easy to fall into traps such as buy now, pay later schemes. Our society in general is already geared to more debt than ever before and our children will probably perceive debt as completely normal. When we add to this the fact that our children may not have a secure career – their income may not be assured – we start to feel very concerned for them.

The population is also ageing, which means that as our children grow older, the burden on them as a group to support an elderly population will increase. This will also affect their job prospects and put more pressure on their finances.

Against this backdrop, we, as parents, are faced with the challenge of how to teach and train our children to be responsible with and understand money. We all know that if we start very early and establish good savings habits and an understanding of the costs of debt, we can instil appropriate values around acquiring material goods.

As we saw in Chapter 1, attitudes and habits about money are learned at an early age. Very young children begin to learn about money by watching the way in which their parents approach money issues. They notice whether parents argue or discuss calmly how money is to be spent, who pays the bills, and who keeps the records. This will have a subtle but significant influence on how they feel about money throughout their life. We need to really look at the example we set; how we make money decisions and how we discuss money at home.

Are you teaching your children sound money habits?

Try this quick quiz to help you evaluate what you are doing to teach your children sound money habits for life.

	Yes	No
Do my children earn some money which is theirs and are they able to make decisions on their own?		
Do I avoid using money as a reward or punishment?		
Do I set a good example? Do I manage my money effectively, pay my debts and so on?		
Do I discuss money management and decisions with them?		
Do I help encourage comparison, evaluation and information gathering prior to spending?		
Do I give my children more financial responsibility as they get older?		
Do I allow them to make mistakes related to money and help them understand the consequences?		
Do I praise them when they make good money decisions?		
Do I match the dollar value of their savings?		

A majority of 'Yes' answers indicate that you are helping your child learn money management skills. A majority of 'No' answers could mean you need to help them a little more.

Helping your children learn good money management

Cecily Moreton is a psychologist, and Director of Moreton Executive Coaching Pty Ltd. Cecily discusses how children learn from their parents and what we can do to help this process.

How do children learn financial skills from their parents?

Children learn both explicitly and implicitly from their parents. Children usually copy behaviour from those they love and admire. They will take on board the messages — for example, 'Always save for a rainy day', 'Grandpa Fred is a spendthrift', 'Choose the item that's on special', or 'Always buy good quality so it lasts'. If there wasn't enough money to go around so everything earned had to be spent each week, the child may continue spending everything they earn even if, as an adult, they earn a high salary. By contrast, children who are brought up in a 'saving culture' are rewarded for saving — they may have bank accounts which they see accumulate and then they are rewarded with their goal.

Teaching children to save, even if it is ten cents in every dollar, is an important lesson. Teaching children to budget their savings is a very useful learning exercise. For example, put in place a system to set aside enough from each week's pocket money to save for a realistic goal, some for fun now, and some for family birthday gifts coming up during the year.

What can parents do to encourage saving?

The way we modify another person's behaviour is by applying consequences. The best way is to agree on realistic and meaningful consequences, and then apply them. Punishment rarely works well — the person who is punished just stops the undesired behaviour for a little while and feels resentful. 'I told you so' is a big dampener, and the child will later associate negative feelings with the whole issue of money. It is much better to be encouraging and build a positive relationship with the child and praise them and reward them with agreed positive consequences when they achieve goals.

Pocket money is important, but I think many parents misunderstand pocket money – they position it as a payment for 'good behaviour' and use it to punish 'bad behaviour'. Parents should think about repositioning pocket money from payment to something more in line with a sharing in the family's wealth. As children get older they take on more responsibility, more freedoms and more pocket money.

Younger children can learn as well. In addition to receiving reasonable pocket money, they can earn more for extra jobs. There can be extra rewards for keeping your room tidy, for a whole week, or being the washing up champion for a week and so on. Explain to them that they are growing up, and therefore their share in the wealth will increase. Let them see, understand and get the rewards for this.

Cecily's tips

- Set a good example – actions speak louder than words.
- Be consistent in your approach.
- Encourage and explain how you are managing your money – involve your children in decisions and activities that are appropriate.
- Help them manage their allowance or pocket money – self-discipline is valuable.
- Talk to them about the spending decisions they wish to make.
- Find ways to encourage children to save. For instance, match what they save with a contribution from you, or promise to add to their savings once they have reached a specified goal.
- Look at the difference between money to spend and money to save.
- Let them make mistakes – let them take responsibility for a poor choice and learn from the experience.
- Help children become savvy shoppers – by reading labels, gathering information and evaluating whether what they are buying is good value.
- Discuss your buying decisions – explain your thought process and reasons.
- Credit involves responsibility as well as privileges – if your child needs to borrow money set a definite repayment schedule.

John is now in first-year university and talks about how he learnt to save as a young child.

I grew up as a 'Dollarmite' kid. I had a bank account and I would put in my 20 cents each week and watch it grow. I enjoyed the numbers adding up and I would talk to my parents about what I was going to buy. When I was 16 my parents gave me $500 to put in the account to help me start saving for 'Schoolies Week' and university. I worked hard and watched my account grow and managed to save nearly $1000 by the time I finished Year 12. I had enough saved to go to Schoolies Week and have a little left over. I now need a car and so Dad has lent me some money and has drawn up a contract of repayment. It's an interest-free loan as long as I pay it off at a regular agreed amount. If I fail to meet the repayments then interest is charged. I think that I really learnt a lot about having a goal and then putting money aside each week towards that goal from when I was small. I now find it quite normal to do this.

Saving, rather than receiving something as a gift, also reinforces the value of money. It develops the idea that if you have a goal you can gradually save and achieve it. It's dangerous for children to believe that they can have all their desires fulfilled straightaway – better for them to experience delayed gratification, so that they have realistic expectations of how long it will take them as adults to acquire the things they need or want.

Structuring pocket money is another technique you can use to help children understand how much they are spending. Some parents even start a budgeting process and devise a method where parents will pay for things such as infrastructure and home costs such as food, health and school, and the children save and pay for everything else – this includes clothes, gifts, toys and their share of holidays.

Another important value about money is the notion of self-reliance. If children grow up believing that their parents will always bail them out of trouble, they will be much less likely to develop financial responsibility. It can be a fine line to tread, not wanting your children to come to grief, but letting them make some mistakes so that they have the experience and the expectation that they can solve their own problems.

Developing strategies for shopping with children

Shopping strategies can be developed for children. These may include things such as searching and researching for the best price and value. One way to show children how to drive their pocket money further is to do some price comparisons on different alternatives and help the child make the decisions about what to buy and where to buy it from.

This exercise can be very valuable as children learn that similar things are actually priced very differently – there are variables, such as location, shop, brand, and so on, that may alter the price significantly even though the quality may be similar.

Another area where children are easily swayed by aggressive marketing is the demand for expensive brand name shoes and clothes. No amount of rational explanation that one pair of joggers is much the same as another, at least in terms of function, will persuade a teenager to go for the cheaper option. With older children and teenagers, set a clothing budget. Give your child reasonable freedom to choose what they want within that budget (and within other constraints, such as wearing a proper school uniform on school days). Then it's up to the child to decide – for example, five chain store T-shirts, or one designer T-shirt. If they would rather wear the same designer T-shirt every day, that's their choice. It's all part of growing up and making financially responsible decisions.

A variation on this theme is for parents to set a fairly basic clothing budget, with any designer extras to be paid for out of pocket money or a part-time job.

Below are some examples from us of how we shop with our children:

Frances
When I buy clothes for my oldest daughter (aged 10), we have a rule that we both have to agree on everything we buy; we shake hands on

every purchase, and she promises to wear the item in question. There is no point in me buying anything without her; if she doesn't like it she just refuses to wear it and it's a complete waste of money.

Dianne
When I'm out shopping with my 12-year-old daughter and she sees something she wants, my first response is always, 'How are you going to earn it?' She can use her pocket money, or earn it through extra jobs.

Di
My four-year-old son is a sucker for any type of collectable toy; whenever we go into a shop with these toys on the counter he will throw a very public tantrum if I say no. Most of the time I'm prepared to look like a terrible parent and resist; it can be very embarrassing. I'd like to say my response is always consistent but every now and then he'll catch me on a bad day and I'll give in.

Emily
The constant 'I wants' never cease from my oldest son and to compensate for this, he now has to save for most of the gimmicky toys or fads that come our way. If it is an expensive item, we will pay half and he makes up the other half. He has started asking for jobs to do around the house and this is really encouraging. At Christmas, he and a friend set up a lemonade stand. I made cookies for them to sell — they sold the lot and pocketed $25 each!

Jobs – how they can help children develop values and discipline

Earning money teaches your child a sense of freedom and recognition, financial independence, work standards and habits, how to evaluate job alternatives, and how much effort is involved in earning money.

Many young teenagers start work by babysitting, lawn mowing or working in fast food outlets. As they get older you can help them by encouraging them to get some training – even if it is a bar course so that they can get a job in their teens. This will also teach them that certain skills are required before you can get a job – it is quite difficult to just get a job completely unskilled. There are also chain stores and food outlets that have quite impressive training programs for their young employees. Most teenagers who do the programs say that this training really helps them learn a lot about the workforce, managing people, dealing with difficult situations and also about earning money.

There is a risk that teenagers become so besotted with making money that they try to take on more and more paid work, to the detriment of study. It's important to set limits on the number of hours they work. In the long term, studying will be more beneficial to their financial future than working an extra shift at their casual job.

Jack did a training course and worked after Year 12 to save money to go overseas.

I did a bar course and worked in a bar for six months after I left school. The bar course helped me get the job in the first place – I certainly couldn't have mixed cocktails and carried the glasses if I hadn't done the course. My parents paid for the course and it was well worth doing. The whole thing was a good experience for me. It gave me real motivation to gain more skills and I realised that working in a bar was pretty boring and very tiring work. I knew that I didn't want to do that for the rest of my life and so it was a good lesson to learn early.

With a bit of planning and some lifestyle adjustment, you can cope with the financial strains of having children. With what you have learnt over the years, you will then be better equipped to teach your children about money and help them gain financial independence. Our children *will* grow into adults and it is our responsibility to equip them with the tools they need to have an enjoyable and fulfilling life.

CHAPTER 11

Being prepared

Being prepared for the unexpected is an important part of financial fitness. It can save you a great deal of money, as well as emotional anxiety. Being flexible and prepared in case you lose your job, having the appropriate insurance cover in case you get sick or burgled, and making sure that you have a will are all part of the process of being prepared and are all important to your financial wellbeing.

The impact of the economy on your income and expenses

We are all affected by the state of the economy both in Australia and globally. The economy affects our income and our ability to change jobs or start businesses. If you are self-employed, the state of the economy will have an impact on how much you can sell or how much you can charge for the services you offer. If you are an employee, the performance of the company you work for will directly affect your salary and your future prospects, including a pay rise and chances of promotion. Keeping an eye on changes in your industry sector is important, as it may give you an early warning sign that it is time to start looking for another job or perhaps selling your business.

The health of the economy will also affect your expenditure. The cost of living, including rent, food, health, education and transport, is affected by general economic conditions as well as government policy. Interest rates also go up and down depending on economic forces – as they change, your mortgage repayments could increase or decrease significantly. By watching these fluctuations you will be more prepared for changes that can affect your income or expenses.

In general, when the economy is doing well there are always more job choices and pay increases are more likely. When there is an economic downturn or slowdown, organisations often cut jobs and stop pay rises. The economy runs in cycles – interest rates, prices, salaries and the general level of economic growth move up and down. Watching and understanding the broad cycles will also help you be prepared.

Your job and career

The state of the job market influences the type of job you can get, your future career potential, and the way in which you are employed (e.g. as a permanent employee or as a contractor). The job market is made up of a number of different industry sectors; each sector is affected by the ups and downs of the economy and sometimes world events. There are regional differences too; where you live will affect what work is available.

An example of the way in which the world economy has affected parts of the job market in Australia is the effect of international terrorism on the tourism and hospitality sector. If there are fewer people travelling, the industry cuts back its services and also its staff. Jobs are cut, and there is also less money to pay those who manage to hang on to their jobs. These changes may affect businesses operating across the whole sector, including airlines, hotels, restaurants, tour operators and many others. All these factors will affect your income-earning potential.

The changing nature of jobs and the labour market

The shape of the labour market is changing dramatically and as workers, our choices and expectations are affected. Full-time, long-term employment is now becoming rare. Employment opportunities are moving to more flexible work arrangements. Jobs are no longer for life and so making sure you are flexible and prepared to change jobs or employment type is now very important to your financial security. There are whole sectors that did not exist a few years ago and there are now far more people undertaking what are sometimes called portfolio careers. A portfolio career is a series of different types of work, often in different sectors. In a lifetime most people will have a number of different jobs in a a number of different organisations or locations. This is in contrast with the past, where traditionally many people started and trained for one career and continued this until they retired, often staying with the same organisation for their whole working life.

It is now very common to find people undertaking work such as:

- Project work
- Freelance work
- Task work
- Casual and part-time work
- Fee-for-service positions e.g. some doctors
- Fixed-term contracts

Understanding what will be best for you is important in preparing yourself for financial security and income-earning potential over the long term.

Joanne worked in a large corporation for a number of years before starting her own business and becoming a contractor.

I work as a consultant for a number of key clients. I sometimes undertake large projects for them or I may just work a day or two a month for them on a specific issue or project. It gives me the ability to leverage my skills and work with a range of different groups and perspectives. I feel much more confident doing this than relying on just one employer to give me work. If I lose a client, I still have a number of others to work with. I guess the downside is that if the companies I work for cut back all at once, I will need to look harder! But I am confident about my skills and what I have to offer.

In the workplace, there are also changes in the way work is organised that affect the type of work we do. The traditional job description of having one major task and responsibility is changing to multiskilling. This means that you will probably be required to undertake a range of functions and responsibilities. There is much more focus on performance and productivity, and overall most people work longer hours.

This means that you need to prepare yourself and ensure you have skills and attributes which are flexible enough to meet the future needs of your organisation – or that you have portable skills to take to another company. Most people will probably face the challenge of changing job types or perhaps work location at least once in a lifetime. You may have a choice or you may feel forced to make a change. Though changing jobs can be scary and sometimes daunting, it can also be empowering and open up a whole new area of interest.

Protecting and improving your career options

There are many books, websites, sections in newspapers, and so on, which will give you a great deal of information about starting, changing and developing your career. It is important to keep reviewing your career and your choices to maximise your financial security. Reviewing what is happening in various industries will give you information about how the industry sector you are working in is performing, average salaries in similar jobs, as well as career options and prospects. You will see from reviewing these that some industries pay more than others. For example, banking and finance institutions pay more on the whole for the same job as compared to those in the health sector.

Relative salaries do not necessarily stay constant over time. When demand for certain skills increases so does the salary – similarly, when demand is low salaries usually fall. For example, when the telecommunications industry became overcrowded, many people employed in the IT sector found that their wages fell and there were fewer jobs available.

Ask yourself the following questions to assess your current position:

- How secure is your current job?
- How secure is the future of your particular industry sector?
- Is it possible for you to get a promotion?
- Do you enjoy your job and work for someone you respect?

Tips

- Check daily newspapers – they often have articles on specific jobs, sectors and geographical locations. They also have specialist career sections which have feature articles especially on job prospects and changes in the marketplace.
- Look for special programs on TV, as well as watching the news for information on the economy.
- Look in specialist magazines.
- Search on recruitment web sites. These websites also have helpful job hunting tips that apply to most occupations. Try www.mycareer.com, www.seek.com and www.monster.com
- If you go to a recruiter, try to be as clear as you can about what you want, and why. Even if you really aren't sure, at least come up with a few alternatives to discuss.
- Make a list of 10 companies you'd like to work for, and why; this exercise will help clarify your objectives.

Our career stories

Dianne worked for a large merchant bank as a management accountant. When she became pregnant she stopped working and decided to try to get more flexible work arrangements so that she could spend time with her new baby. As a chartered accountant, she has specialist skills which are transportable. She was approached by a few people she knew to run training programs such as financial skills for non-accountants, and she developed this business over a number of years. When her daughter grew older she took a role as a management consultant.

Frances is also a professional – she is a lawyer. She worked for a large company and then started her own practice to give herself more flexibility while her children were young. Recently she has returned to working as an in-house lawyer with several organisations as a contractor.

Emily juggles a number of roles as a self-employed copywriter. Her pattern of work could be described as a portfolio career, taking on contracts and project work. She has matched her work against her time commitments to raising her two boys.

Di has also had a portfolio career and she has managed to map her career against countries she wished to work in and areas of interest. She has found that by continuing her education and studies and remaining flexible, she has been able to pursue a range of roles in different but related sectors.

There are some common themes amongst us. We all have tried to retain a balance between work and our family commitments. We always seem too busy and have too many things on, but we try hard to work on our priorities and keep our goals clear. Because we have children, need to work, and want to enjoy our lives, we recognise that we need support. Our network of friends and colleagues gives us support, ideas and help – much the same as some formal clubs offer. Our regular investment club meetings, for example, provide us with an easy way to not only discuss investments, but also to raise issues and problems that we are facing – whether it be issues at work, how to find a new job, problem clients, how to manage things at home, or how to study as well as juggle everything else. This group is an important network for us and provides a point of reference outside our home and work for us to bounce off ideas, get feedback and in some cases gain a better focus.

We have found that expanding and keeping a good network of contacts is important not only to stay informed but also to get feedback and in some cases to find new jobs and clients.

Barrier busters

- Check and ensure your skills are up to date.
- Watch what is happening in your industry and field.
- Join your relevant association and look for networking opportunities.
- Keep your CV up to date.
- Ensure that you have balance in your life – look at how much leisure time you have and how many activities you have organised with family and friends.
- Try to stay fit and healthy.

When to ask an expert and get some professional support

Whether you are starting out in your career, assessing your current position or thinking of or being forced to change jobs, it may be useful to get some professional support and advice. Career advisers and career coaches offer valuable services. Centrelink provides some services and has information on a range of occupations. There are also career reference centres in most cities and numerous websites.

A typical career counsellor will help you review your career in terms of the following categories:

- Lifestyle
- Interest
- Income

A career counsellor will usually review choices against a job/occupation database to review options and potential outcomes in the three categories. They will look at demand in the sector, job potential and growth, salary expectations, ability to maintain flexibility and other factors.

Sessions with some counsellors – particularly those at school – are often free. If you are seeking a private professional, they can cost anything from $30 to $200 a session. Career counsellors are listed in the phone book, or you could call the Australian

Association of Career Counsellors (1800 222 390) or the Australian Psychological Referral Service (1800 333 497) to find a counsellor in your local area.

Dr Susie Linder-Pelz is a career coach and owner of Good Decisions Pty Ltd. Susie talks about how a career coach can help you.

My work as a career coach is with empowering people to take charge of their lives. Many people are looking for a career change and are not sure what to do; others have been retrenched and need reassurance.

It is important to find out why you are not satisfied with your current position or to really look at what and why you want a particular job right at the start. Most people go straight into action – they start looking for a job! My view is that this is not the best approach. We need to go through and work out what we want and what we are looking for first – before jumping into action and job search mode.

I work with people to enable them to look at a range of options – for now and in the future. I explore with them what motivates them. I give feedback during this exploratory phase and I generate options for the client. Once we have established the options that fit, I coach them in the process of evaluating their options. We come back to the specifics of job titles, careers, sectors, locations and other information.

Susie's tips for anyone assessing their job and career

1. Understand what motivates you
2. Explore and evaluate your options
3. Look at what is required to handle change, then
4. Work through the processes to resolve any limiting beliefs and fears – this is about changing the limiting beliefs to empowering beliefs. This is where we go through various processes to look at how to build confidence, moving from fear to courage.

What can you do if you lose your job?

Even with the best planning things can go wrong. Whether we like it or not, at some stage many of us will have to come to grips with redundancy, and its consequences: redeployment or retrenchment. These are the 'three R's' of modern employment reality.

Firstly, what do the three 'R' terms mean?

- **Redundancy** technically applies to a job that no longer exists.
- **Redeployment** means moving an employee to a new role in the same organisation.
- **Retrenchment** is termination of employment resulting from a redundancy.

Losing your job is said to be one of the major stress factors in life – it is right up there along with moving house, divorce and death. For some it can be a real shock; for others it can offer a very positive and sometimes welcome new start and a whole new way of approaching things.

Being prepared can cut down on financial pressure as well as emotional issues. For instance, having enough money saved to live on for three months will give you breathing space to sort out your finances and start looking for another job. If you do get retrenched then you quickly need to reassess your spending habits and do your Money Picture in Chapter 3 again. You will need to work out what you are going to have to spend money on and what you can cut out until you get your income stream back on track.

Claudia's retrenchment came as a complete surprise, even though she was working on a successful piece of business. She suddenly realised that was not enough, particularly when large companies decide on cost-cutting measures.

I was in my late twenties and working for a prominent advertising agency. I loved my job and each day was a challenge.

Then one day my life took a dramatic turn. Rumours of recession abounded, and the advertising industry was laying off people every-where. Eleven people were retrenched from my agency and I was one of them. I had been working on a successful account; I couldn't believe it because my account was generating good revenue for the agency.

I never understood why my job became redundant, even though my work colleagues tried to console me by saying it had nothing to do with work performance. All over the world my agency had to make staff cutbacks in each office. Anyway, I found myself out of a job. With my redundancy payout, I decided to have a month off and take a break.

I recall it was a very difficult time, as agencies across the board were also laying off staff. I had to stay positive and look for other opportunities. In the end, what saved me were my networking abilities. I still had many friends in the industry and in time I was able to get back into the workforce.

My redundancy happened a long time ago; at the time I was devastated but it taught me a valuable lesson. I really didn't understand the benefits of networking, until that terrible day. I always tell people to keep in touch with your colleagues and be on the lookout for opportunities.

Losing your job doesn't have to be all doom and gloom. This is a time for a change – even if it's one that maybe you would have preferred to have a little more in your control. We all react differently to change and losing your job may affect you in quite an unexpected way.

If you are made redundant, then normally you will receive a payout, although some recent corporate collapses have left employees with less than their proper entitlement, or no payout at all. It's always a good idea to have enough money saved up to cover a few months' living expenses just in case.

Some steps to help you in the event of losing your job are listed below.

1. *Make sure you know your rights and how much you are owed.* You will be entitled to any unused long service leave (if you have been with the same firm for five or more years) and annual leave, as well as some form of termination pay and of course your superannuation (but you must roll over any 'preserved' element of your super). The federal standard for redundancy

payments is part of most awards and provides around four weeks' notice for people who have worked with the employer for more than four years, plus up to eight weeks' redundancy pay. Some awards and employers will pay more than this, but you may receive less if you are not covered by a federal award. At more senior levels individual contracts are more common and will spell out your severance package. While the employer is bound to provide you with your legal entitlements, it is always worth checking to ensure that you have been covered. Check that you are not able to negotiate for more and that there are no administration errors. You may need to get advice from your union or a lawyer.

2. *Check your tax situation.* Tax on a redundancy payout is calculated differently to your normal pay in that you will receive concessional tax treatment. You will (based on 2002/2003 figures) receive the first $5623 tax-free plus pay no tax on an extra $2648 for each year of service. For information on the tax treatment of redundancy or termination payments you should contact the Tax Office.

3. *Understand and plan your finances.* If handled well, this payout may provide you with an unexpected sea change in your life. This may be the time that you can actually reassess what you have been doing and start to do what you really enjoy. It is important, however, to understand how much money you should receive and how much you need to run your life, as well as review your investment options. Taking stock of your financial situation at this point is important. Things that you need to consider include:

- What do I owe?
- What do I now have to pay for that previously the company paid?
- What are my weekly and monthly expenses? Can I still afford these?
- Redo your Money Picture – look at all your regular payments and work out which ones you need to continue and make sure you can cover these.

Be honest and open with your partner and family. This is a situation that affects you all and it is better to discuss the options honestly and openly. You may need to go through the things that you can no longer afford or the things that have to go on hold.

If you do not have enough money to cover your outgoing expenses while you look for a new job, make an appointment to see your bank or financial institution as they will be able to work through some options with you to cover you in the short term. Many recruitment companies also provide some financial information. Of course, if you can get access to a financial adviser then they could also give you some other options. Assess all your options before you do anything. Although it may seem like you have a great deal of money, plan out your expenses before you go buying a new lounge or booking a holiday.

4. *If your company doesn't provide it, it may be worth seeking a session with an outplacement service or career counsellor to get another perspective on your future options, boost your skills and support you in your planning.* These organisations will help you do practical things such as prepare your résumé, help you research and work out the best way to search for a job, and help with interview techniques and practice sessions.

5. *There are some government assistance plans and you can find out about these through Centrelink.* There is also a support system for retraining offered through the New Enterprise Incentive Scheme (NEIS). This scheme offers ongoing business advice and also some financial assistance.

Being prepared is a good start and will help you feel more confident as you contemplate and work through your next move. Our most important financial resource is our ability to earn money. All of us are vulnerable to the ups and downs of the economy that affect our workplace, how we work and what opportunities we have. The only certainty is change, so try to be proactive and get your career in shape to strengthen your financial fitness.

Maintaining a balance

We believe in trying to achieve a good balance in our life between work, family and leisure. Because we have families, work, study and have a desire to keep fit and healthy, we have become jugglers of time and priorities. We are confronted with the pressures and conflicting priorities of work, family and trying to care for ourselves and keep ourselves happy and healthy. We believe that health, fitness and having a balance in our lives are of critical importance. We see our health as our most important asset. We all do different things and these things depend on how much time we have, where the children are at in their school and life and how much support we can get from our partners or others.

Frances goes to the gym regularly and walks almost every day. Dianne walks to work most days and does yoga and boxing. Emily likes to walk and keep fit. Di swims or runs at the beach most days and tries to do yoga a few times a week.

We also put a lot of time and effort into family and our friends. We all value these aspects of our life and do not believe that any job or any amount of money can take priority over these important things. They give us our reason for living and our motivation.

Insurance

Being adequately insured is another important part of your financial fitness regime. Sometimes, things happen that are out of our control – natural disasters, illness or theft. This is where insurance comes in. You work hard for your money and if you then lose the things you have worked hard to acquire, through a burglary, fire or other disaster, or you don't have an income because you get sick, then this is the same as money just draining out of your bank account. Insurance is about managing your risk. It is about being prepared for unplanned and unscheduled events. In this section we look at the most common types of insurance and what to look for in a policy. We will help you review whether you need a particular type of insurance policy and also help you critically assess policies on offer.

What is insurance and how does it work?

The business of insurance is the management of risk. Insurance companies agree to take on the risk of various accidents or disasters that might happen to you, and you pay them to do this; the payment you make is called a premium.

Over time, the insurance company must collect more in premiums (and income earned on investing those premiums) than it pays out in claims. So it researches the likelihood of the insured events happening, in order to set the premium at a level that will produce a profit. It can seem like a bad deal for you as a consumer, paying out the premium every year and knowing that it's unlikely you'll ever get any of it back. But thinking that way ignores the huge financial mess you'll be in if something disastrous does happen and you are not covered.

Insurance is a *basic ingredient* of financial fitness. It's critical that you insure your important assets (including yourself!) adequately.

Some forms of insurance are compulsory, such as third party policies attached to vehicle registration, to compel every driver to accept and pay for his or her fair share of the risks of being on the road. But most insurance is voluntary. There are various events you can and should insure against, and there are traps you have to watch out for when taking out a policy.

Building and contents insurance

These are quite separate insurance products; although often bundled together, you can have one without the other. Building insurance is relevant if you own a house. If you live in a flat that you own, you won't have to worry about it directly, as insuring the building is a communal expense and the cost is included in your levies.

If you own a house on its own title, the responsibility to take out building insurance is yours. Most importantly, if you owe money on the property, the terms of your mortgage will stipulate that you must keep your building insurance current until the loan is fully paid off. The reason for this is that if your house burns down, for example, or is destroyed in an earthquake, you would be left with an asset worth the land value only, and this might be less than the amount you owe to the lender.

Building insurance only covers the cost of replacing 'fixtures', i.e. the structure of the building itself. It won't cover replacement costs of furniture, appliances, computers, clothes, etc. These are all covered by contents insurance.

Contents insurance is more expensive than building insurance, because claims are much more likely to be made. Renters need it as much as owners do, because your landlord's insurance does not cover your possessions.

Make sure that you have the right amount of building as well as contents insurance. If your home burns down then you will need to replace both.

Always read your policy thoroughly and make sure you check all the boxes.

Car insurance

It's compulsory to take out insurance as part of your vehicle registration to cover you in the event you injure someone in a car accident. This leaves two forms of voluntary insurance: vehicle insurance and third party property insurance. Comprehensive insurance is a type of policy that includes both vehicle and third party property insurance.

Vehicle insurance covers the cost of replacing or repairing your car if it is damaged or stolen. Premiums vary enormously, depending upon the age of both the car or motorbike and the driver, and on where (or whether) the car is garaged. Many of these variables are things you won't have much control over. All you can do is shop around for quotes.

There are two ways of defining the amount you will be paid out for a replacement vehicle: market value, or a defined value. The latter is a better bet, as the insurance company's idea of market value is unlikely to coincide with your own.

These days, insurance policies are written in plain English, and are reasonably easy to understand. Make sure you find out about all the circumstances that might stop you from being able to make a claim – for example, if the car is stolen and you have left it unlocked.

Third party property insurance covers property damage (as opposed to personal injuries) caused by your vehicle. It covers all property damage, not just other cars, but it won't cover damage to your car. So if you drive your car into someone's fence, or their house, the insurance will cover the cost of repairs.

In her job as a lawyer Frances saw how this worked in practice. She came across many court cases where an insurance company pursued a property damage claim against a motorist. These cases came about because the insurance company had paid out on a claim from its insured driver, who had been in an accident that wasn't his or her fault. The insurance company would then take the driver at fault to court to try to recover the amount of the claim.

The insurance companies, through their lawyers, could be very persistent. They had judgment entered against the driver at fault, and then tried to have their assets seized. If the driver applied to the court to pay the debt off by instalments, the insurance company's lawyer often opposed the application, and at the very least tried to get the instalments set at the highest level possible.

Many of these drivers were on low incomes, with their own car not worth insuring, but they'd had the misfortune to damage an expensive car. The cost of repairs could run into many thousands of dollars, and to add insult to injury, the insurance company would add interest and court costs to their damages as well.

Even if your own car is not worth insuring, third party property insurance is relatively inexpensive, especially when you think about what might happen if you run into a brand new Mercedes.

Life insurance

This is the only form of insurance that is guaranteed to pay out eventually. There are two types of life insurance policy: endowment policies and term policies.

Endowment policies are becoming less common. They include an investment component, which can be cashed in at any time during the life of the insured. However, the premiums are high, and in the past, fees and commissions were high too. Endowment policies were more popular in the days when you needed a large lump sum to invest in a managed fund, as they were a way to invest small amounts on a regular basis. These days there are many managed funds that allow you to do this, with lower and more transparent fees.

Term life policies are simple; you pay a premium, and if you die while the policy is current, the insurance company will pay out the nominated lump sum to your dependants. The amount of life insurance you need will depend on the needs of your dependants; they will want a lump sum big enough to pay off your debts, replace your income through investments, and hire outside help to carry out the household tasks you used to do.

The cost of term life insurance is dictated by your gender, age, and whether you smoke. You may also be asked to disclose your own and your family's medical history.

Some term life policies also have a 'trauma' element, where they will pay out if a defined traumatic event occurs, such as you being diagnosed with a terminal illness, or suffering a heart attack, stroke, etc.

Disability/income protection insurance

If you get a financial plan drawn up by a professional financial adviser, you'll find that income protection insurance is likely to be included in it. This is because the plan will depend on you being able to earn a certain level of income over the next 10, 20 or more years, and if you can't earn that level of income due to illness or injury, you will be left high and dry unless you have this kind of insurance.

There are huge differences in the varieties of disability/income protection policies on offer. You really need to get into the small print to find out exactly what's covered. The main area of contention is the type of 'disability' covered by the policy.

Some policies will only pay out if you're unable to work at any occupation. So if you are a concert pianist or a surgeon, and you injure your hand, the policy will be of no use to you, because there are still plenty of jobs you could do, even with your injury. This type of policy will only pay out if you are very seriously injured or incapacitated, so much so that you can't do any job at all.

Other policies will pay out if you are unable to carry out a job for which you are qualified. For example, if you are a builder, and you hurt your back, the policy would pay out even though you may be capable of doing work that is not physically demanding, such as office work. However, if you are a manager, with a job that is mentally but not physically demanding, the policy won't pay out if you can still do clerical work after your accident or illness.

The best policies are those that pay out if you are unable to carry out your usual occupation. Even in this category, there are important differences. For example, some policies will pay out only if you can't carry out a defined set of duties required by your job, regardless of whether or not you've suffered a reduced income as a result. Other policies will pay if your income is diminished as a result of your disability, regardless of what duties you can or can't perform.

Some income protection policies will only cover you if you work full-time, or if you spend most of your working hours inside an office. So it's extremely important that you find a policy that covers your individual situation exactly at the outset when you take out the policy, and review it whenever your working situation changes or you get a letter from the insurance company at renewal time saying they want to change the wording.

Income protection policies are particularly important if you're self-employed, because you won't have access to workers compensation. It's compulsory for employers to take out workers compensation for their employees – however, the benefits are restrictive (you can only get a proportion of your previous salary). For that reason, even if you are an employee, you should look at taking out extra cover in the form of income protection insurance.

Some company superannuation schemes provide income protection. Check your superannuation policy and your coverage to make sure that you are not covered twice and that your coverage is adequate.

Health insurance

There are two questions to ask yourself here: do I need health insurance at all, and if so, when should I start?

The advantages of having private health insurance are:

- Access to private hospitals. Some private hospitals can guarantee you a room to yourself, or just sharing with one other person. The surroundings are usually more luxurious than in a public hospital, and the food is better.

- Being able to choose which doctor will treat you.
- Shorter waiting times for some elective surgery.

The disadvantages of private health insurance are:

- It's expensive, with full hospital cover costing from about $600 per annum for a single person and $1200 per annum for a family.
- You might still have to pay a gap if your hospital or doctor charges more than the amount agreed with the health fund.
- With most types of medical emergencies, requiring very high levels of medical care, you'll end up in a public hospital anyway.

There are two types of health insurance: hospital insurance, which basically covers treatment in private hospitals, or as a private patient in a public hospital, and ancillary cover, or 'extras', which covers other expenses such as dental, optical, physiotherapy, etc.

The federal government has set up a number of financial incentives and penalties to encourage people to take out health insurance. The first incentive, in the form of a penalty, is the higher Medicare levy that applies to high income earners who do not have hospital cover. Single people with a taxable income of over $50,000, couples who earn more than $100,000 and families with incomes greater than $100,000 (plus $1500 for each child after the first) pay an extra 1% Medicare surcharge – in addition to the 1.5% Medicare levy all taxpayers pay – if they don't have hospital cover. (To escape the surcharge, you must take out hospital insurance where the excess is not more than $500 for a single or more than $1000 for a family.)

The second incentive is a scheme known as 'lifetime health cover'. This scheme makes health insurance more expensive if you delay starting it until after the age of 30. If you take out hospital cover over the age of 30, for every year you delay, the health fund can charge a higher premium, compared to those who started their health insurance before they turned 30. (People who took out hospital cover by 15 July 2000, no matter what their age, are treated as if they'd joined by the age of 30. Also, special provisions apply to those born on or before 1 July 1934. They can take out hospital cover at any time without paying a loading for joining later in life.)

The insurance products themselves, especially the hospital products, are very difficult to compare. There are different excess levels, and different exclusions. For example, you can choose a policy that excludes childbirth expenses, which will lower your premium. The Australian Consumer Association's website (www.choice.com.au) has a helpful guide to comparing different health insurance products.

Some argue that private health insurance is unnecessary, and you'd be better off to put aside the money which would otherwise be spent on the premium and invest it yourself. This takes some discipline; you have to be sure that you really will invest the same amount of money every year, and it has to be in an easily accessible investment in case the worst does happen. Even so, you should at least take out ambulance cover (usually included in hospital policies). It doesn't cost much as a separate item, and could save you a vast amount if you were ever in an accident, especially if it happened in a remote location.

Health is unpredictable, and you could be truly grateful one day to have private cover, as Jill's story shows.

When I was 35 weeks pregnant with my first child, I was diagnosed with high blood pressure. I tried to stay at home and rest completely, but my blood pressure kept going up. My doctor told me I should be in hospital for the rest of my pregnancy, so that the baby and I could be constantly monitored.

So instead of having a week in hospital, I was there for nearly a month. The cost was astronomical, more than $400 per night, but thank goodness it was covered by my insurance. If I hadn't had insurance, I would have been forced to go to a public hospital. No doubt a public hospital would have given the baby and I a good level of medical care, but I was extremely grateful to have my own room, nicer food, and peace and quiet in the private hospital. These things count when you're in hospital for a long time.

Mortgage insurance

Unlike all other types of insurance, this is one type of insurance policy you should avoid if you possibly can. Mortgage insurance doesn't protect you as the borrower; it only protects the lending institution involved.

You'll most likely come across mortgage insurance when you buy your first house or flat. If you're borrowing more than the lender's limit (usually 80% of the purchase price), the lender will insist as a condition of the loan that you take out mortgage insurance. If you default on the repayments, the lender can call on the insurance, and then the insurance company will come after you to recover all the amounts it paid out to the lender.

The premium for mortgage insurance is set as a percentage of the amount borrowed, and is payable in a lump sum. It might be paid in a lump sum, but the amount is usually added onto your loan, so you are paying it off, with interest, over the life of your home loan. Mortgage insurers are very conservative in the types of property they will cover; for example, they will often not cover studio apartments or warehouse conversion developments. It can be heartbreaking to find out that your dream property, at the very limit of what you can afford, is knocked back by an insurance company and therefore out of your reach after all.

There is absolutely no benefit to you in taking out mortgage insurance, other than it possibly being necessary for you to get a start in the property market. Try to avoid it by scraping together a higher deposit, or shopping around for a lender with a higher lending limit.

Travel insurance

There's only one thing to say on this topic: anyone who sets foot outside Australia without it is taking a crazy risk. If you can afford to travel, you can afford to take out travel insurance. The time to take out the policy is when you pay for your trip, as cancellation expenses are sometimes covered in certain circumstances (check the fine print as usual).

Six questions to ask when taking out a policy (and to keep in mind for the duration of the policy)

With all types of insurance, as well as making sure that the policy will cover your particular situation, you have to watch out for the traps that can stop you from making a successful claim if the worst happens.

1. AM I COVERED FOR PUBLIC LIABILITY? Public liability insurance protects you from legal liability caused by your negligence. Examples of this type of liability are:

- You are having a party at your house and one of the guests crashes through the railing on the balcony.
- A tile flies off your roof in a storm and injures a passer-by.
- Your dog bites the postie.

Building insurance should cover liability resulting from the state of your property, e.g. the balcony or the flying tile scenario.

Contents insurance can cover liability outside your home, such as a biting dog on the footpath.

You should cover yourself for $10,000,000.

2. IS THERE A CO-INSURANCE CLAUSE? This is a particularly nasty loophole that can be buried in the policy wording. A co-insurance clause says that if you have underinsured your building or contents, and make a claim, the insurance company only has to pay out on the policy the percentage equal to the proportion you have insured for.

For example, the replacement cost of your house is $200,000, but you have only insured it for $100,000. The house is completely destroyed by fire. The insurance company will only pay out $50,000, i.e. half the amount insured. How can they get away with this? The reasoning is that by only insuring for half the true cost, you have agreed to 'co-insure' for the other half, i.e. you have agreed to bear the risk of half the replacement cost yourself.

3. DOES THE POLICY PAY ME THE REPLACEMENT OR THE DEPRECIATED VALUE?
Most people would assume that their contents insurance will pay
the replacement value, i.e. the cost of buying brand new items to
replace those which were stolen or destroyed. Not necessarily! This
is something to watch out for, because for items such as clothing,
the difference between replacement and depreciated value (i.e. the
value of the item second-hand) is enormous.

4. WHAT ARE THE EXCLUSIONS? This one is pretty obvious. Insurance
policies always have a list of exclusions. Some exclusions are
surprising – flood, for example, in building policies. Insurance
companies are constantly updating the exclusions in their policies,
terrorism being a good example of a recent addition.

5. HAVE I DISCLOSED EVERYTHING RELEVANT? You have a duty to disclose
to the insurance company anything that may be relevant to its
decision to accept your application, even if the application form
doesn't specifically ask. This is a continuing obligation, not just
when you're taking out the policy. So if you've been storing petrol
in your basement, without disclosing this to the insurer, and the
house burns down, your claim won't get very far. (Of course, if you
told the insurer about this up-front, your application for insurance
probably wouldn't get very far either. You'll need to minimise the
risk yourself first, then tell the truth.)

6. WHAT ARE MY CONTINUING OBLIGATIONS? It's not hard to void your
insurance policy by accident. For example, with a standard
building policy, you must:

- Keep the property secured and in good repair
- Not leave the property unoccupied for a specified period of time
  (usually 60 or 90 days)
- Not make any admission of liability (i.e. admit that the loss was
  your own fault) without the insurer's consent

Each type of policy will have its own particular ongoing obligations.
We've only covered the more common forms of insurance in

this section. There are others: for example, loss of rent (if you have an investment property), domestic workers compensation and credit card insurance. The principles are always the same if you're shopping around for insurance – read the policy carefully, make sure you know exactly what is and isn't covered, and make sure that you have disclosed everything relevant to the insurer. Remember, you can always shop around for insurance. If the policy doesn't pay out when you need it, it will have been a complete waste of money, and a setback on your path to financial fitness.

Wills and powers of attorney

You could be surprised at how much your estate is worth. Even if you haven't bought a house or car, you'll have other assets. Not having a will can create a major financial burden, not to mention being a bureaucratic nightmare for those you leave behind. All that you have worked so hard for may be at risk.

At various times in the past, when a person died, their precious possessions were buried with them. Things have changed, and unless you're a pharaoh (and we're going to assume that you're not), having a valid, up-to-date will is an important part of keeping control over your finances. If you don't have a will, each state has laws that set out a formula for distributing your assets after you die. It's a tedious and expensive exercise, and can create real financial problems for your family or loved ones.

Making a will is reasonably quick and inexpensive – coming to terms with your own mortality is the hard part. Often it takes a prompt such as buying a property to make people finally get around to it.

Frances' experience is typical of most lawyers who work in this area.

When I was a lawyer in a small suburban practice, I prepared quite a few wills. Most commonly, people would have them done when they bought a house, or got divorced, to get all their legal affairs sorted out at the same time. The vast majority found it quite a relief to get their will over and done with, and planned only to review their wills if their circumstances changed.

A small minority changed their wills frequently, cutting out various friends or family members, then often reinstating them in the next round of changes. One client admitted to me that his aim in making a will was to control his family from the grave!

What exactly is a will?

A will is a written statement where you set out what you want to happen to your assets (also known as your estate) after you die. You can make a new will as often as you like, and every new one will override the previous wills. There is no standard form as such for making a will, but if you follow the legal technicalities it will be much easier for those who inherit your estate (i.e. your beneficiaries) to prove the will and put it into effect. If the will has not been worded, signed or witnessed properly it might not be valid. You should always make sure that your will appoints an executor, whose job is to make sure that the property is distributed properly and in accordance with your wishes.

When should I make a will?

- When you first start to earn money. You could be surprised at how much your estate is worth. Even if you haven't bought a house or car, you'll have other assets – cash, employment entitlements, superannuation, the proceeds of life insurance (often included in your super).
- If you marry. Marriage revokes any prior wills. This means that once married, your previous will is automatically cancelled and if you die, your estate will be treated as if you had no will at all. There is one exception to this rule, which is that a previous will continues to be binding if it explicitly states that it is made 'in contemplation of marriage'.
- If you divorce. Getting divorced will automatically revoke any provision in your previous will in favour of your ex-spouse. The rest of the will is valid, but it might not operate properly; for example, you might have to appoint a different executor.
- If other circumstances in your life change. For example:

— You start or finish a de facto relationship.
— You have children.
— A person to whom you previously left money dies.
— You come into a lot of money.
— You want to appoint an extra or different executor.
— You go into business.

All these circumstances are events that should trigger a review of your will.

What's the best way to get my will done?

Most wills are prepared by lawyers. If your will is straightforward, the lawyer will work from a precedent (i.e. standardised) document, and the cost should not be great; not more than $150 to $250. It is usually possible to negotiate a fixed professional fee with the lawyer.

Trustee companies also prepare wills at no charge, in return for a commission that comes out of your estate after you die. Using a trustee company is worth looking into if there's no-one you can trust to act as your executor, because the company will take care of all the administration. Make sure to find out exactly how much the commission will cost before you decide, as it is calculated as a percentage of the total value of your estate, and can run into many thousands of dollars that would otherwise go to your beneficiaries.

You can make your own will, using a form from the newsagent or the post office. There are risks in relying on a home-made will, partly because the rules for signing wills are very technical, and partly because it's easy to inadvertently put something in the will which is unclear in its meaning.

I want to make a will but don't know what to put in it

The first decision to make is who will be your executor. You can appoint more than one executor, or you can appoint alternatives; for example, you can appoint one or both parents, or if they die before you, a brother or sister. It's a good idea to have at least one executor who is younger than you, so they are more likely to outlive you.

Next you have to decide whom to leave your assets to. You don't have to leave specific assets to different people; instead you can divide your estate into shares and leave different percentages to different people. This is especially useful if you are young, because at the time you are making your will, you really have no idea what assets you'll own at the time of your death, hopefully a long way into the future.

It's a good idea to have alternative beneficiaries appointed, in the event that one of your beneficiaries dies before you and you don't have a chance to make a new will. This is not pleasant to contemplate, but say, for example, you and the beneficiary are in an accident together.

If you have young children, think about leaving some or all of your assets to them via a 'testamentary trust', in which those assets are controlled by a trustee until the children reach a specified age. There are tax advantages, in that the income from money invested in a testamentary trust is taxed at the normal income tax rate (unlike children's normal investment income, which is taxed at a punitive rate). Also, you might want some of your money to go directly to your children rather than have them depend on inheriting from your partner.

Watch out for the legal rule which says that if two people die at the same time, the older of them is deemed to have died first. The following is a hypothetical example.

A married couple make wills in favour of each other. They have no children. The couple are killed in a car accident. As the husband is older than the wife, she will inherit his estate under the terms of his will. The gift in her will to her husband is invalid, because the husband is deemed to have died first. In fact, the wife's whole will is invalid, because there is no surviving beneficiary. The wife's estate is distributed according to the laws of intestacy; if her parents are still alive, for example, they will inherit the whole estate, effectively both the husband's and the wife's. The husband's family will get nothing.

The way to overcome this problem is for the two wills to provide that if one spouse does not survive the other, half the estate will go to the wife's family and half will go to the husband's family.

Joint tenancy/tenants in common

Another legal rule to watch out for is joint tenancy, which is a form of co-ownership. When you buy a house or a unit with another person, you have to nominate whether you will be joint tenants or tenants in common. The decision you make will have substantial implications for your estate.

If you own your house (or any other asset) as joint tenant with another person, you can't leave your share of the house to anyone in your will. If you die, your share of the property automatically goes to the surviving joint tenant. If you want to be able to leave your share of the property to someone else in your will, you must own the property as tenants in common. If you are already joint tenants, and want to change to tenants in common, you will have to sever the joint tenancy. The procedure for doing this varies from state to state; ask at your local land registry office.

I've made my will – who should I tell?

The contents of your will are completely confidential until you die. There's no need to tell anyone what's in it. The original should be kept in a safe place such as a lawyer's safe custody system (which is usually free), or bank safe deposit box. It's a good idea to store a copy separately to the original. It's also a good idea to ask your executor if he or she is willing to act; if not, it would be better to find someone who is happy to be appointed. Even then, you don't have to give your executor a copy of the will or tell them what's in it, if you don't want to. Just let your executor know where the original is kept.

Granting a power of attorney

Now that you're thinking about making a will, why not think about granting a power of attorney as well. A power of attorney is a document in which you appoint someone to be your attorney – i.e. that person can sign documents on your behalf. Anyone can act as an attorney, as long as they are of sound mind and over the age of 18.

The power can be limited or unlimited in scope. For example, you can limit the power to only operate inside a particular time-frame, or only to apply to a specified transaction. The advantage of appointing someone to be your attorney is that they can deal with your affairs if you are unable to; for example if you are ill, or overseas. Obviously, the person you appoint must be completely trustworthy.

You should have the power of attorney prepared by a lawyer. As with wills, it is usually a standard document and the lawyer should be able to quote you a fixed fee. Often it's a good idea to register the power of attorney at the local land registry office – essential if you want your attorney to deal with real estate on your behalf.

Lisa's brother asked her to be his attorney while he lives overseas.

My brother and his partner have gone to live in Japan for a few years. They've each appointed me as their attorney. Although they've set up most of their finances, including their bank accounts, so they can be operated from Japan, every now and again something will come up where I need to use the power. For example, when the owners' corporation for their flat holds its annual general meeting, I can use the power to grant myself a proxy and attend on their behalf. Luckily for all of us I haven't really had to use the power very much at all, but it has given them enormous peace of mind to know that if something did crop up, I would be able to sort it out for them without urgently having to rush documents all over the world.

To cancel a power of attorney, simply notify the attorney in writing (and if registered at a land registry office, lodge a written revocation at that office).

If you've already made a will, you've done well. But do check to see if it's up to date. Maybe there are some changes you want to make. If you haven't made your will yet, jot down some notes on what you want to go in it, and then make an appointment to get your will drawn up while it's still fresh in your mind.

Avoiding scams and con artists

Over 100,000 Australians have lost money to a scam over the past 10 years – don't be the next one!

As we are advocates of building wealth, the last thing we want to do is put you off investing. But there is another side to investing that requires some attention, and that is to be aware of scams and con artists. Armed with enough knowledge you will be able to sift through the myriad investment choices and know when it's safe to venture. The fact is that anyone can get caught out so it's worth discussing some of the likely traps that are out there.

Falling for an investment scam is like spraining your ankle before the big fun run you've trained long and hard for. It's not planned and causes pain and suffering that can take weeks to mend, just as recovering from an investment scam can take you years to get back on track. To protect yourself from any scam, you'll need to keep your ears and eyes open. If you have ever watched one of those current affairs shows, then you won't be surprised at the number of people who get caught out in these 'get rich quick' investments. Once you hear their stories, you wonder how could they have let it happen.

But it's not just the needy or destitute who are preyed upon, as no-one is immune from the 'scam artists'. Professionals, retirees, and mums and dads have all been targeted and succumbed to the allure of these so-called investments.

You may say, how could this happen? Why didn't they protect themselves? We are going to help you wise up to the con artist.

In reality, this section could be a whole book, so numerous and ingenious are the number of scams and despicable acts played out by con artists in their attempts to make a buck. The good news is that there are organisations that are out there to help and protect you. You may have heard of the government organisation called the Australian Securities and Investments Commission (ASIC) and thought, 'That's just for companies, not for me.' Before you part with any money to invest anywhere, check out the ASIC website at www.fido.asic.gov.au. Information on scams is easy to get from the ASIC website. For any first-time or serious investor, it's worth a visit.

As a consumer you are also represented by the Australian Consumers Association (www.choice.com.au). Once you log on, go to their money section for practical advice on how to protect your hard-earned money, as well as how to make the most out of your investments, mortgage, and credit cards, to name a few.

The other way to protect yourself is by following this three-point protection plan. It's common sense and simple to remember.

1. Take time to look beyond the promise

There's a wise saying that is worth keeping in the back of your mind: 'Anything cheap will cost you in the end.' Look beyond the glitter and hype and check out if there really is any money to be made.

Tips

- Do not be pressured into signing up straightaway.
- Take a friend or family member with you. Tell them not to let you sign anything while you are there and use them as a sounding board.
- Ask yourself what you want to get out of the investment. Where else can you get that information? Is it easily available and free?

2. Ask questions – it's your right

Get as much information as you need and ask questions before you hand over any money or make a commitment.

If you ask questions and do not get an adequate response, then your internal alarm bells should start ringing, particularly if the person appears to be dodging your questions. If they cannot answer your questions on the spot, they should be able to get back to you at a later time with the information.

If you are offered a money back guarantee, find out what conditions have to be met to get your money back.

3. Check out the facts before you sign anything or hand over any money

By this we mean asking professionals – your lawyer and accountant. You could include your friends, family and work colleagues. People you trust, who will look at the investment objectively as they are not emotionally involved. Be wary if you are being asked to sign something immediately. You may be told that you will lose out or miss out on a great opportunity. The reality is that the time you take to consider all the issues involved could save you in the end. And, of course, check out the websites we have spoken about earlier.

The bad guys exposed

Here are some scams to be aware of (you may have heard of them):

- The investment seminar
- Illegal managed investment funds
- The cold callers
- Queensland property
- The Nigerian scams
- Lottery wins

THE INVESTMENT SEMINAR We have all received them in the mail or seen them in the newspaper: the 'investment seminar'. These are the 'get rich quick' schemes promising 'wealth without work'. For most of us this creates massive appeal in that there is a quick and easy way to achieve quality of life. You start thinking, 'If others can do it why can't I?'

These catchy and alluring brochure headlines are aimed to get you hooked:

- 'You can become a millionaire in three years.'
  (Really? Well, why aren't you doing it instead of running these shonky investment seminars?)
- 'Traditional investments are too slow and lack excitement'
  (Ever heard of risk versus return and investing in blue chip companies over a 10-year period?)
- 'You can turn your financial dreams into reality.'
  (Whose financial dreams are we talking about, yours or mine?)
- 'Amazing, unbelievable strategies for building massive wealth.'
  (Sounds like body builders' dodgy protein powders.)

ASIC says on their website: 'In our experience most of these seminars push dangerous strategies, such as borrowing huge sums of money to buy property, unusual investments or shares. Some are simply scams.' They describe the atmosphere as: 'Seminars are psychologically super charged. People in this motivational, emotional atmosphere aren't in the right state of mind to make sensible investment decisions. What's being offered isn't value for money. Some seminars can cost $10,000 for a weekend. You have to ask yourself if you're getting value.'

PROPERTY INVESTING SCHEME FOR DEPOSIT BONDS There are plenty of versions of the investment seminar. A common version is the property investing scheme for deposit bonds. A deposit bond is where you buy into a property under construction for 1% of the purchase price rather than the normal 10%.

The strategy is to buy a number of properties off the plan (i.e. before construction is completed) using multiple deposit bonds, often on the same day. The properties are then on-sold before completion, and the only up-front cost to the investor has been the cost of the bond and stamp duty.

Think about what happens when the property does not increase in value, interest rates rise and you are left to pay a settlement for which you don't have the money or the ability to borrow it.

THE ILLEGAL MANAGED INVESTMENT FUND There are many legal, well-managed investment funds available in Australia. There are also illegal managed investment schemes, which are among Australia's worst investments.

In a well-managed investment scheme:

- Your money and other members' contributions are pooled together to provide a financial benefit to the members.
- You and other members give up day-to-day control over the operation of the scheme to the professionals.
- The scheme is registered with ASIC.

An illegal investment scheme is best described by the absence of what a legal one must have:

- A registered managed investment scheme must set up a *public* company that is registered with ASIC on its public database of Australia's 1.2 million companies.
- A registered managed investment scheme must get a licence in the company's name to 'operate' the scheme.
- A registered managed investment scheme must register the investment with ASIC as a 'managed investment scheme'.

The reasons for not registering a scheme generally fall into two categories: some illegal schemes are started by well-meaning but incompetent people who don't know the law and have no idea what they are getting into. They get a bright idea to make money, but they do not have the skills and systems to manage other people's money efficiently, honestly and fairly.

Shady, dishonest people start other illegal schemes. They operate outside the law because it's easier to cheat you when they don't have to follow any rules. This can be a hard one to protect yourself against, because it's usually 'sold' by a family member or a community group, where you trust the person telling you to take up this great opportunity. It appeals to our sense of wealth without work.

THE COLD CALLERS Our tip for dealing with cold callers is hang up and hang up and hang up again . . .

You may have seen a news report on the 'boiler rooms raided in Bangkok'. In your mind is a vision of a number of people sitting in tiny cubicles with phones in a grubby, pokey office. These people are employed to cold call you and introduce themselves as an overseas broker from a company. ('The Kensington Group' is one of the names that ASIC has identified as phoney brokers.) They are not investment experts or brokers. They are trained to use high-pressure sales tactics to talk you into buying shares.

Common with other scams, they offer a 'unique opportunity' with 'huge returns'. Then they offer to transact the deal for you and all you have to do is send the money to their brokerage account. Of course, no shares are bought and your money goes into an account where it may be impossible to get back again, depending on the legal and supervisory system in the country your money has gone to.

QUEENSLAND PROPERTY A cold caller invites you to attend a free seminar. At the seminar you will hear about the tax advantages of negative gearing. These are legitimate Tax Office expenses where you claim your interest on money borrowed and other expenses as a tax deduction. If your expenses are more than your total income from the rent on your investment property, you can deduct the shortfall from your other income. (See Chapter 7 on building wealth.) The disadvantage is that high-pressure tactics are deployed to get you to buy a property for much more than its current market value.

At the seminar you will be coerced into a free trip to 'see for yourself' the property in Queensland. Usually you'll be shown a very nice unit set back from the beach that can be purchased for a small amount. However, if you did your homework and went to the local real estate agent, you will see that similar units are much cheaper when they are marketed to locals.

Look past the salesman with the shiny white shoes, the all-over tan and grin from ear to ear, as pressure is applied to get you to sign up for the purchase. While you are up there you'll hear lines like: 'You will lose this great investment if you don't sign today. This is the last unit. We have another buyer who's going to sign on it tomorrow.' Remember, take time to look beyond the promise, ask questions, and check out the facts before you sign anything.

This scam is particularly targeted at Sydney or Melbourne, where people are not familiar with the local Queensland market.

THE NIGERIAN SCAMS This one has been around for a while and has received a considerable amount of press. Nonetheless an unbelievable US$5 billion has been handed over to the scamsters from victims all around the world.

The scam involves getting a letter, fax, or increasingly an email, asking for your help in transferring money out of a country (in the past often Nigeria, but now we see South Africa and Afghanistan featuring too) because of its political instability. They usually have really good official-looking letterheads and promise to pay you a huge sum or 'reward' just for sending your bank account details and a small amount of money to cover expenses to transfer the pot of money out of the country to you. As ASIC points out, this is just the beginning: 'Once you're hooked, you'll be asked to pay all sorts of "advance fees" (e.g. customs, taxes, bribes) to facilitate the transfer. These fees are the real purpose of the scam, and may add up to tens of thousands of dollars.' Never give your bank account number or other personal details to unauthorised people.

LOTTERY WINS This scam usually appears in the form of a registered letter addressed to the owner. Typically, it reads that you have won some money in an overseas lottery. To retrieve your winnings you must send money across to the scam artist. The amount can vary from $25 to $100. Of course, once you send your cheque or money order, you will never see your winnings. Steer clear of anything that says you have won the lottery, unless you have actually participated in one.

Here is one that Frances came across. It's a beauty!

I've found a wonderful scam example – it came in the post addressed to my husband; they must have got his name off a mailing list somewhere. It's a very glossy brochure advertising 'investment software', and it goes on at great length about wouldn't you like to earn an extra $70,000 a year, etc? Nowhere does it explicitly say, but you can work out that the software is for betting on horses. They say something like, 'The TAB pays out $X billion dollars every year – now you can share in this massive payout.' It's just amazing. They describe it as 'investing in thoroughbreds'! I'm tempted to ring them up and find out a bit more, like how much it costs, which is obviously not mentioned in the brochure. But I'm scared I'll have their marketing staff harassing me for the rest of my life.

Investing your hard-earned money in legitimate avenues is essential to build wealth and secure your future. Once armed with our three-point protection plan, you'll have enough information and confidence to expose any scam you come across. Don't forget, if the peddlers who push these schemes really knew how to get rich quickly, they would do it very quietly and not tell a soul!

Our message to you

If there's one message to take with you from this book, it's this: anyone can be financially fit. Just as the most unfit person can become physically fit, you don't have to be born with any special talent to achieve financial fitness. All you need is the will to succeed, and the discipline to get on the right track and stay there.

We know that taking control of your finances can be hard to do, because we've all been in that situation ourselves. We procrastinated, thought we didn't have time, thought it would all be too hard. We needed inspiration, and in the end it came from each other. Through our investment club, we discovered that learning about investing can be interesting and fun. We found out that ordinary people can learn about the basics of investing, without having to do any special courses or study anything too technical.

These days, we are still juggling our careers, families, friendships, hobbies and interests. Our investment club is still going strong, and is a fantastic source of encouragement and support for us. We are not perfect, and our plans go off the rails from time to time. But we are definitely more committed and focussed than we were five years ago. We have managed to turn around our negative attitudes to money and finances, and you can do this too.

To build on the theme of finding inspiration from others, we spoke to other people who faced the same barriers that confront all of us, and overcame them. These success stories are from ordinary people; none of them have put their achievement down to good luck or to having had some innate advantage. The common thread that binds them is simply that they have focussed on their finances, identified the problems that confronted them, and worked out how to fix them. Where they've needed a special skill or knowledge, they've paid for the right adviser to provide it.

For both financial and physical fitness, there is no magic transition, no giant leap. Rather, fitness comes gradually, over a sustained series of small steps. There will be some milestones, when you know you're on the right path – the credit card paid off; the first investment into shares, managed funds or property; the moment when your Money Picture moves from Red, to Amber, to Green.

When you are physically fit, training is not as much of a struggle as when you first started to exercise; it becomes more and more enjoyable as you get stronger and set higher challenges for yourself. Achieving financial fitness is much the same; your confidence increases as you start to see results, and managing your money becomes increasingly enjoyable. In both cases, it doesn't matter what shape you were in to begin with; what counts is getting started, setting your goals and working out how to achieve them.

It might sound like constant dedication and deprivation, but we certainly like to go out and spend. We want to have fun, and that's the whole point: if you're worried about money or if you can't control it, spending it will make you feel guilty and anxious. The aim is to be in control of your money and, as a result, to enjoy it more. We know that money can't buy happiness, but it can go a long way towards giving you more choices in life.

Now is the time to overcome any underlying negative attitudes you might have about your finances. Resolve to get over whatever excuses you have used in the past. Bring them out into the open, have a good close look at them, and then discard them. Think about the people you know who have got their finances under control, and the people who have shared their stories with us in this book. There is no reason why you cannot do exactly the same as they have done. You already have all the skills you need; all that's left to do now is to put them to use.

You can contact us via our website: www.themoneyclub.com.au

Ten principles of financial fitness

1. No matter where you are now, you can improve your financial fitness. You don't need to start with a lot of money.
2. Getting started is the most important thing – set aside half an hour today.
3. Don't expect everything to always go 'right' – we all go off the rails sometimes. The important thing is keep at it.
4. You do have enough time – it's about making time.
5. Knowledge is the key to overcoming fear.
6. Look to your friends, family and colleagues for help and inspiration.
7. Don't forget to protect what you already have.
8. Motivation comes from knowing exactly what you are working towards. Write down your plans and goals to make them real.
9. Remember you can't do everything alone. Get the right professional advice.
10. Keep in mind why you are doing this: to have more fun and achieve your goals!